necessary
evil

VOLUME II

Kareem (INFINITY) Hayes

Copyright © 2016 Kareem J.Hayes
Published by: I.N.F.360Inc.

All rights reserved. No part of this publication may be reproduced, stored in a retrieval system or transmitted, in any form, or by any means, electronic, mechanical, recorded, photocopied, or otherwise, without the prior written permission of both the copyright owner and the above publisher of this book, except by a reviewer who may quote brief passages in a review.

The scanning, uploading, and distribution of this book via the Internet or via any other means without the permission of the publisher is illegal and punishable by law. Please purchase only authorized electronic editions and do not participate in or encourage electronic piracy of copyrightable materials. Your support of the authors rights is appreciated.

Designed By Vince Pannullo
Print by: One Communication. 800.621.2556
Printed in the United States of America

ISBN: 978-0-9983972-0-7

CONTENTS

DEDICATIONS

NECESSARY Evil volume 2 is dedicated to the memory of my deceased grandmother Rosetta Hayes, my aunt Martine, and my grandmother Irma Cleophat. All of these women have loved me unconditionally and guide me from the great beyond. To my Queen Natasha who has been my back bone and support system throughout the entire writing process.

To my son Malachi Hayes whose youth and tenacity has empowered me to push harder. Last but not least this book is dedicated to New York's Jamaica Queens community for embracing me. Thank you all.

PROLOGUE

I T'S all quite sickening; the beginning, the ending, and every ugly detail in the middle. Somehow, despite the forces that seem to hold you down, you get up. We grow, we take it.

We are all guilty of it. We are all guilty of being materialistic. Who doesn't want the latest Jordan's or the freshest shoes? Or maybe your desire is to have a great home; a sanctuary for your loved ones—nothing too extravagant, just a little short of a palace. Well then, how far would you go to obtain worldly comforts?

At the root of man's primal nature are the need to survive, and the need to multiply and be fruitful. On rare occasions men surpass the social norms and become great. These men are labeled heroes, icons, gods, villains, devils or even stars!

Despite the many differences we deal with as humans because of race, gender, religion, culture, etc., there is something we all have in common, and that is necessary evils. We have to serve man's primal needs.

This nation was founded on necessary evil when Europeans colonized America. That was a "necessary evil". When wicked politicians make decisions to invade and violate people's rights that is a "necessary evil". So, is a politician who takes money under the table more innocent than a young girl stripping to pay her college tuition?

I don't know one Black man with a plane. I don't know anyone in Bed-Stuy or Harlem who owns a cargo plane or a cargo boat. So, not to sound cliché, but who is bringing drugs to the urban communities throughout America?

When your back is against the wall and you face the extreme opposites that rule our reality; when the options are live or die, eat or starve, fight or fall, rich or poor. When you must dig into the dungeons of your soul and invite an inner demon to avenge you; a person becomes accustomed to the fear of starving and dying. This is such an ever-present reality that a person develops a kind of psychological callus, becoming a sociopath. Emotions exist, but they must be suppressed because they are a sign of weakness.

So when we explore the term "necessary evil", let's bear in mind that no one is without sin. Even the devil was a child of God, so let's not judge. Let's rejoice in the downtrodden who rise above the ghetto swamps of poverty and degradation.

Welcome back to my universe where the sun revolves around a big rotten apple that Eve took a bite of. The subway trains are the worms that travel through the apple. If the trains are the worms, what does that make us? Oh, I know. We are the parasites in the belly of the beast. We are the bacteria needed to help break down, process and digest all the crap that America consumes. We are the scapegoats, the boogie men, the cannon fodder, the pawns in the game. We are the artists that America claims leads kids down an unruly road. We are the poster children for crime, even though the biggest crooks don't wear baseball caps, white V-neck T-shirts and designer jeans. The real crooks wear suits with button down shirts and power ties.

We make the styles; we just don't profit from it. We make the music and the dances; we just don't make the money. The entire American economy was built on slavery, and its new millennial offspring "privatized prisons". We are America's "necessary evil".

CHAPTER 1

POWER

IT was one of those eerie nights in Jamaica, Queens. The rain-drops seemed to tap dance on the pavement. The pungent scent of sour diesel marijuana moved through the air.

One-hundred Sixty-Fifth Street between 89th and Hillside Avenues is where the legendary Hut Barbershop is located. It is a place that has become sort of a landmark in Jamaica, Queens where brothers from all over the area come to get groomed and talk "new stuff" and engage in debates ranging from who is the best, Naz or Jay-Z, or who is going to the NBA finals.

The regulars frequent the barbershop on this night. A variety of brothers pass through: gangsters, schoolboys and family men alike. Even celebrities come through and mingle with everyday people.

50 Cent's song "You not Like Me" blared out of the speakers inside the barbershop:

"...Momma said everything that happens to me is part of God's plan,
So at night when I talk to Him.
I got my gun in my hand.
Don't think I'm crazy 'cause I don't fear man,
But I fear when I kill a man,
God won't understand..."

It was a Friday night, about 10:00 p.m. All the stores on the Ave. were just about to close.

Lee, the barber, kept the shop open a little late so he could finish off some of his customers.

Polo, a well-known stickup kid from the neighborhood sat in Lee's chair. He was getting his usual haircut; a low and dark Caesar with a slight taper.

In this concrete jungle, Polo was a predator; vicious and effective. His nickname "Polo" came from his old school "lo-life" days when he was part of one of New York's most notorious street gang. He was what you would call a "taker". Anything he wanted, he took.

He was old school, with 14-K gold fronts to hide his missing front teeth. He got his stocky build from doing over fifteen years in prison. Call him a dinosaur; the last of a dying breed

The dinosaurs of New York's concrete jungle are now becoming extinct. Groups like Zulu Nation, the 5-Percent Nation and Latin Kings had an element of cultural awareness. These were organizations that lost their way. It used to be about protecting our communities, not terrorize it. The older groups struggled to fit into the mold of the "new" New York street culture.

The ever changing trends in society seem to affect the streets. Every day a new gang pops up, and the criminal code of honor is diluted until it has dissolved. There is an immense disconnect between the older and younger generation, both pointing at each other, and neither embracing a more holistic view of our communities.

In urban America, each generation had to bear the burden of its predecessors' sins. When you have fatherless sons fathering sons, you have generations and generations of people who lack the information and knowhow to stop the cycle of genocide.

******

Elmo sat low in his black tinted out Nissan Altima. He was parked up the street from the barbershop. He had been sitting there waiting for about two hours.

Elmo was a unique young man. He had the charm and charisma of a salesman, but the cutthroat mentality it took to be a hired assassin. He was skinny with a long, thick neck and a strong round jawline. He had beady eyes that earned him the nickname Elmo. Like the "Sesame Street" character, he was named after his fluorescent smile that could light up a room. Being the type of person who could smile and laugh through some of the worse circumstances, no one would suspect that he was a murderer.

******

Polo sat in the barber chair, loud and obnoxious as usual, gloating about his exploits with multiple women, while Lee, the barber somehow masterfully found a way to multitask. Lee conversed with Polo while maneuvering the hair clippers to cut perfect angles as Polo yapped away. It was like painting on a moving canvas.

"…Yeah, son, the bitch that works at Footlocker on the Ave.," Polo was saying.

"What chick?" Lee asked.

"The manager. A redbone bitch with them big titties."

"Oh, yeah. Oh yeah, I know her. She's a'ight," Lee said.

"Shorty's a jump-off. I had that bitch licking my balls. Word, she a freak!" Polo continued.

The music was loud, the mood was festive, and all the guys in the shop were drinking.

Elmo casually walked in smiling and shaking hands as he walked through the shop. Walking over to Lee in a non-threatening manner, he said, "Yo, pardon me, son. Let me talk to you." He then pulled the barber away from his work and locked eyes with him.

Polo must have picked up on Elmo's vibe. Elmo reached into his jacket pocket, Polo instinctively felt for his own gun in his waistband. Unfortunately for him, he left it in his car. Polo was physically stronger than Elmo and just might have been able to overpower him and wrestle the gun from his hand, but he lost time in the split second he was reaching. He did manage to hit Elmo with a staggering right hook while hopping out of the barber's chair, and ripping the smock from around his neck as he dashed towards the front door.

Elmo spun out of the blow, knocking over Lee's clippers, scissors and other barber paraphernalia.

The entire barbershop was in a frenzy, and everyone hit the floor for cover while the dazed young nineteen year old gun for hire shot three precise bullets that lodged in Polo's back, stopping him dead in his tracks. His body stiffened up before he could grab the door and escape.

Grinning, Elmo then walked over to finish his kill. As he was walking, he spoke out loud to Lee and the remaining barbershop patrons. "Alright, now when the police get here, y'all better say niggas robbed y'all, and were wearing masks." It wasn't a warning; it was a death sentence delivered with a grin. "Because if the police come and pick me up, I will have my goonies at your house, ready to murder ya fucking kids!" His Nike Airforce One's crunched through the broken glass and debris.

Polo lay there frozen, hearing Elmo's footsteps while his annoying voice in the near distance mixed with the rain pouring outside and the music pumping out of the speakers. All the sounds meshed together to become a beautiful requiem as the "Angel of Death" approached. Polo's mind wanted him to move, but he was paralyzed from the neck down. All he could do was breathe and brace himself for the end.

Elmo casually walked over to his victim and placed the barrel of the .44 caliber Desert Eagle on his head. "Okay, turn over, O.G. Open ya mouth, nigga. Let's make this easy," he said.

"Fuck you, little bitch!"

"Oh, see, I'm trying to be easy."

"Fuck you!"

Elmo let off three more shots straight into Polo's facial area pointblank. After he shook off the smoking gun, he quickly walked to his car and sped off.

When he got to a stop light he ejected the clip and reloaded his gun, because if he happened to get pulled over, he had no intentions of going peacefully.

As Elmo drove, he got a call on his Samsung cell phone from a private number. "Yo, who dis?" he answered.

"Did you take care of that?"

"Yes, I did, Big Homie. Tightened his ass right on up!"

"Good. Get low, change up ya outfit and come see me for some paper."

At the other end of the phone was Supreme. Supreme had moved his operation to Jamaica, Queens. The wars in Harlem made them too noticable. Supreme had his own connections in Queens. He continued to work with Pistola, but he managed to amass a small army of young bloods who were eager to build an enterprise. Supreme ruled with an iron fist, and anyone who turned against him or tried anything remotely offensive would be made an example of, like Polo.

Supreme was obsessed with power and would do anything necessary to get it.

Chapter 2

C.M.K./P.N.A.

THE climate of New York City had changed. Long gone are the days of baggy jeans, Champion hoodies, and Timberland chukkas. Now is the era of fitted jeans and European influenced fashion. Hip-hop's golden era has given way to a more melodic and southern based rhythm. Once upon a time New York City was a place full of originators. Recently, it has become the hottest part of the melting pot; an actual amalgamation of styles and music from all over the world.

Neighborhoods like Harlem and Jamaica, Queens, which consist of predominantly Black, West Indian and Latino communities, had developed pockets of Caucasians moving in. The rents have skyrocketed. Apartments that used to be $500 to $800 a month are now $1,000 to $2,000.

Lady Liberty was war-torn and scarred post 9/11. The Twin Towers fell, and so had the economy. The recession is in full effect. Ten years had passed since September 11, and the world was still feeling the shockwaves of a "new" New York.

Crews and posses of the old days—like the 5-Percenters, Zulu Nation, Lost Boys and Lo-Lifes—have given way to gangs like Crips, Bloods, Young guns and Young Bosses.

It has been more than a decade, and the more things change, the more they stay the same.

Guys like Supreme and Pistola are dinosaurs compared to this new breed of thug. As dinosaurs, they have two choices: adapt or become extinct.

Supreme adapted well. He quickly became a very respected man throughout New York City. His bloodlust and ruthless style of enforcement made him notorious in New York's underworld.

After things got crazy uptown in Harlem, Supreme made a power move out to Jamaica, Queens. The war with the Deadly Lion Posse had been getting hectic. In the aftermath, he had been warring with them for over a decade, and had escaped several attempts on his life.

Despite being Freedom's right-hand man, he was unable to familiarize himself with Freedom's connects. So for a while it was Supreme and Pistola taking on all comers.

Supreme systematically set out to recruit young guys to be under him. Along with the young guys from Queens and a couple of ex-cons that he bidded with, he had amassed a small army. He called them C.M.K. (Cash Money Kids), a continuation of what he and Freedom had started. The guys in C.M.K. preferred to call themselves "Kitty Gang".

Supreme never reconnected with his family. The streets became his immediate family. He still stayed with Chyna, who had a son for him. His son, Supreme Jr. was a brilliant six year old, whom Samaya would babysit on a regular basis.

The new C.M.K. was a vicious group of young men—monsters, in fact. Supreme wasn't their leader. He was more of a big brother/mentor. He would front them the drugs, and they would work it off.

As much as Supreme witnessed it, he could never understand the whole Kitty Gang name. Even the style of this generation was so different. Now the young guys wear their pants and tops fitted. Baggy clothes are over for New York City. Supreme was just past 30 years of age. It was just so weird to him, because he was watching things change around him while adapting at the same time.

Kitty Gang had no leader. They were more like a raging pack of wolves, and the one with the most kills became the "alpha male" until someone with more kills dominates or loses a fight.

Every night the Kitty Gang boys would be on the corner of 164th Street and 89th Avenue, moving everything from cocaine to E pills, MDMA (molly's), crack and Oxytocin.

Despite their wolf pack-like system, there was still an organized business ethic that Supreme instilled in them. The crew was broken up into job functions: hustlers, enforcers and brains.

Elmo was one of the few brothers who could perform every job function. Hailing from a broken home, he never met his own father. He was an amazing hustler with a silver tongue, able to sell a turd to a toilet. He took drug money and invested it by buying and reselling retro sneakers online.

Elmo was a wiz kid with a strong intellect, and that's what Supreme loved about him. If Elmo was just like Supreme, then his partner Red was just like Freedom. Red never had many words unless it was about money. He was a decent hustler, but he was more of a brain and an enforcer.

Red was only 24 years old; a handsome young man with piercing eyes and a defining scar across his lip, and another across his chest from a gunshot wound. He definitely had his fair share of scars, but he could dish it out way better than he could take it. Red had been a warrior his entire life, catching his first murder at the age of 14. His father is doing life in prison, and all he had was his mother.

Whenever you saw Red, you saw Lex.

Lex was a savvy street hustler who had a mastermind quality about him. He had hooked up with Supreme through Pistola. He used to go uptown to Harlem to purchase bricks of cocaine from Freedom, so Pistola passed him on to Supreme. Through years of good business, Lex and Supreme became close. They made a deal, and Supreme moved his operation to Jamaica, Queens.

Part of the reason Lex and Supreme connected so well was because Lex was an older cat; not yet 30 but far from 20. Lex was also a very crafty person. He was a narrow faced, sneaky eyed guy with long black hair, sharp features, high cheekbones and dark skin. He also had a mouth full of gold teeth. When he spoke, it came with power. Lex was the self-proclaimed man of vision.

Although Supreme was something like their boss, he dealt with everyone equally and fairly. The one thing that he would do to keep the whole crew happy was how he distributed the product. Most bosses in the game preferred to pay their workers a commission, but Supreme had a unique manner of dispersing his drugs. Basically, his concept was that you work *with* him, not *for* him. Rather than have a bunch of crack cocaine spots, he opted to wholesale and created partners to wholesale with him. He used the pyramid business scheme. It proved to be very successful, and through Supreme and his efforts, C.M.K. grew and expanded for ten years' time.

CHAPTER 3

"PISTOLA" MEANS "PISTOL"

PISTOLA has spent the last decade killing for a living. This is a man who never knew his own parents. A normal thing would be to call him a killer, but he is more of a sociopath. Being raised by Sopa, he had been trained and bred to be an assassin.

But this assassin's soul had grown weary at this stage in the game. At the age of 30, Pistola was now beginning to contemplate life. He was tired of the bloodshed and waking up in cold sweats. He could never rest peacefully, so he spends his days medicating himself with weed, liquor, and occasionally a snort of cocaine.

It was hard for Pistola to deal with Supreme, who just had a different character from Freedom. Frankly, Pistola never really trusted Supreme, and after ten years of being right by Supreme's side, he really felt Supreme was a snake.

Pistola's body count was insane, and it seemed to keep growing. He longed for a chance to have a normal life, and perhaps be a family man one day.

His mind would roam back to the days when he felt like Sopa's son. Sopa would take him and Mercedes on boat rides and fishing trips. Part of him admired Sopa for being a father to him, but another part wished that Sopa would have killed him.

Pistola has nightmares about his past, like visions of a lost past life. They appear in flashes…

Sopa stormed into his house, and then he heard his mother's screams and a loud "Bang!" Then all of the sudden there is the deafening silence. Then he heard men walking about. A stranger picked him up, and the rest is a blur…

Fast forward a few years, and he's playing in the sand with his sister (not by blood, but by circumstance).

Pistola never went to school like other children. He spent most of his time at the gun range on Sopa's secluded compound. Pistola was a marksman by the age of twelve. Back then, the Dominican Republic was a dangerous place to live.

Sopa's makeshift parenting was brutal and abusive, but it was all that Pistola knew. Teaching Pistola to be a killer was a way of passing down the family trade…

Sopa's Compound, San Cristobal, July 2nd 1980:

The sun seemed extra hot this day. Armed guards patrolled back and forth, while sexy women of all shades and wearing tight bathing suits walked about.

On the inside, Sopa's compound was a palace. But on the outside it looked more like a fortress with an eight foot high wall with barbed wire across the top, surrounded by one hundred acres of land. There was constant security, and to get in or out of the compound, you had to be cleared at the front gate. Surveillance cameras were in every corner of the compound.

Many guests came to Sopa's home to conduct business, but some guests never left. Sopa loved to torture his enemies, and he believed that fear was greater than respect.

The décor was a Greek motif with marble pillars and countertops. But in the basement, there were cold gray concrete floors, leashed attack dogs and numerous devices of torture.

Sopa's entire compound was self-contained. He even had a mini farm. He preferred to know where his food was coming from because he did not want to be poisoned.

One of Pistola's duties growing up was catching chickens, then killing and removing the feathers. It was all part of his sick training.

Sopa would occasionally bring young runaways from off the streets to his home. The young girls were used for various things, from drug trafficking to sex for sale, while the boys were forced into becoming soldiers for Sopa's empire.

Before Sopa handed over a gun or gave a boy a position, he would have them fight in a gladiator style bout. This was fun for Sopa's crew, the soldiers and dealers alike. Anyone visiting his house would be a spectator.

As ten to twelve boys ranging in ages from nine to thirteen years of age stood in a line, the spectators would naturally begin placing wagers on who would win the gruesome fights. This became a form of weekly entertainment for Sopa's crew, and an excellent way to judge recruits.

Although everyone found this to be a fun time, Pistola would dread these matches because he was always forced to fight the last boy standing, he never lost, and he feared that if he did fail, Sopa would surely kill him for humiliating him.

Pistola still remembers the day he got his name. It was a100 degree day in the hills of Nigua, San Cristobal. The view of the Caribbean Sea put on a light show as the sunlight sparkled on the waves.

Pistola was in the farm area, catching chickens, chopping off their heads and preparing them for the cooks. He heard the hustle and bustle of everyone screaming and placing bets. He knew that Sopa would soon send for him.

Pistola was fed up with fighting, and felt like eventually he would lose.

Sopa was somewhere toward the front of the compound with a group of his constituents. He watched as the last two young boys pummeled one another to a bloody pulp.

The one thing about these fights was that even though they seemed inhumane, many young boys from poverty stricken homes would run away on purpose with the hopes of being picked up by Sopa's crew. It was a guaranteed job with benefits.

Hugo, a big, oversized 12 year old with the strength of an adult male pounded a lanky little boy named Carlito. Carlito put up a hell of a fight, and his punches were fast, accurate and skillful, while Hugo was just slow and sloppy. But he was strong and vicious. Carlito was winning, until Hugo was able to get a good grip on him. Hugo squeezed the screaming child and slammed him to the floor. The momentum caused Carlito's head to gush blood.

Most of these matches didn't end in death, just with a young boy being knocked out. But on that day there was bloodlust in the air. Hugo kicked and punched Carlito until the little boy's frail body lay limp and dying.

For the first time, Sopa saw a little boy that exemplified a true killer instinct, as poor little Carlito just lay there shaking as the last bit of life oozed out of his body. Sopa summoned his clean crew to dispose of the body, and send for Pistola.

Elsewhere in the compound, Pistola was busy at work. First he would catch the chicken as it scrambled around the arm in a frenzy. Once he got his hands on a chicken, he placed it on the floor, stepped on the body using his foot for leverage. You could literally hear the chicken begging for dear life. As the chicken screamed out, Pistola raised his machete high above his head, and with one swift motion, he put the chicken out of its misery. Blood spewed from the neck of the decapitated bird like soda from a bottle that had been shake up a little too much.

Killing a chicken was a skill that took time to develop. The blood must be drained properly from the chicken. Sopa was intended on desensitizing Pistola to blood and death.

Pistola spent at least five hours a day butchering animals. He was numb. In the beginning scene of death would make him nervous. Each splash of hot blood that mistakenly hit his face and stained his clothes would make him cringe at first. However, now it was simply business as usual.

One of Sopa's minions entered the farm area and hollered, *"Ven aca, Chamaquito!"*

Pistola responded to *Chamaquito*. He heard it so much that he thought it was his name. He eased his foot off of the chicken's body and proceeded to walk to the other end of the compound to face his opponent.

Hugo stood there staring at Pistola and his scrawny frame. He grinned as he thought to himself that this will be an easy fight, just like the one with the now deceased Carlito.

Every time the young Pistola went into battle mode, his eyes would squint. He would quickly assess his oppositions. His heart began to race and his eyes squinted even more. He looked down and saw the fresh bloodstains on the ground.

Pistola then watched Hugo's fat frame bounce and poise for battle, and looked around at all of Sopa's soldiers placing their bets on him. His eyes moved to Sopa, and Sopa gave him a nod before shouting, *"Dale!"*

With that single command, the two young combatants charged directly at each other like raging bulls.

Hugo was bigger, stronger and meaner, but Pistola was faster, smarter and more experienced. His first blow was swift and accurate, but Hugo had learned from his last fight. So instead of trying to outpunch Pistola, he grabbed him and used his weight to wrestle Pistola to the ground, smothering him and not allowing him any room for him to gain enough leverage to really strike out.

Deep inside, Sopa truly loved Pistola and seemed concerned, but up until now he had never seen his adopted son fight anyone who really gave him a run for his money.

Pistola tried desperately to cover his face while Hugo pounded on him like an angry ape. All the while Pistola's mind raced to think of solutions, but he was getting lightheaded and blood began trickling from the back of his head. He could feel himself losing consciousness as Hugo's huge bear paw-like fist came crashing down on him, breaking through his guard. Hugo continued to bludgeon Pistola's face.

In his peripheral vision Pistola caught a glimpse of Sopa's disappointment. He also caught a glimpse of a decent sized rock. The key was to grab the rock, but he had to keep his guard up. His forearms were absorbing the brunt of Hugo's onslaught. One direct blow from Hugo might have ended the fight, but it was a risk that Pistola had to take.

Pistola quickly grabbed the rock, but took a dizzying blow to his head that swelled one eye shut and caused blood to gush from his nose. But he had that rock in his hand. With every ounce of strength he had left, he swung a left hook, connecting the rock to Hugo's temple, instantly leaving his right eye bloodshot. It dazed Hugo, but did not stop him.

All that was needed was that brief moment. A relentless attack ensued where Pistola literally bashed Hugo's face in. With each blow he delivered, Hugo slipped further into darkness. Each blow went from a hard, dry shell-cracking sound to a moist thump, as if Pistola went from crushing Hugo's skull to smashing his brains. He was lost in a violent frenzy of adrenaline and survival.

Pistola mounted Hugo and continued to hit him as Hugo's body went into convulsions. It was overkill. Pistola was a violent child with mixed emotions.

Sopa yelled, *"Ya, Chamaquito! Ya!"* bringing his young protégé to a stop.

But Pistola couldn't stop. His young life flashed before his own eyes. He saw Sopa, the only father he knew and whom he loved and hated. At the same time he saw flashes of all the chickens he killed. He felt Hugo's fresh hot blood spatter against his face, and he was surprised that the blood was so much thicker than a chicken's.

Once Hugo stopped breathing, moving and shaking, Pistola rolled over in exhaustion and stared up at the beautiful blue sky. It was peaceful lying there next to his very first human kill. He gazed up and wondered what God had in store for him as those white clouds floated about. It was a surreal feeling that came over him. For a moment it was like he was in the depths of Hell, but he could still look up and perceive Heaven above.

His feelings were confirmed when the beautiful view of the sky was interrupted by Sopa, the devil himself. He stood over Pistola and extended his hand to lift him up. "You did good, *Chamaquito*. That's your very first kill. You did it with your bare hands. Now you're ready to stop practicing on chickens, and start killing men. *Ven aqui*, my little Pistola. Now you are a man!"

From that day on, Sopa began to call him "Pistola" or "Pistolito".

CHAPTER 4

TEARS OF AUSET

MARVIN Gaye's song "Trouble Man" poured out of Margie's headphones as she sat on the bus. This was that long ride to the U.S.P. Federal Detention Center in Lewisburg, Pennsylvania that she dreaded. It is where her son, Freedom (Jamaal) is. Freedom's fifteen year sentence is coming to an end.

Margie hasn't seen her son's face in two decades. They've been communicating through letters. She wondered what her son looked like, and more than that, she felt this insatiable guilt.

Margie was the last of her kind. With ten years clean, she now lived a sober lifestyle, taking it one day at a time. She became a director at Daytop, a well-known drug program. She became one of the most popular counselors years ago, and she quickly rose through the ranks.

Margie managed to pull her life together, but she had a bad case of survivor's guilt. Despite her life going well, she had a ghost haunting her.

Sometimes a resident would come into the drug program, and it would be an old "get high" buddy. It happens like a flashback. When you don't see someone for a long time, their face can bring you back in time.

In Margie's situation, she had a lot of friends who did not make it. Some were victims of violence, and some were slaves to the drugs and couldn't free themselves. Those addicts who walked the streets like zombies are a reality check, because that could have been her. That young girl who caught HIV while selling sex for drugs could have been her too.

So, as a counselor, the chance to help her peers is sort of redemption. She feared that she would not find redemption with Freedom. She feared that it was too late to change the man he had become.

Margie was all too familiar with the nuances of running narcotics. It was a form of chemical warfare bent on deteriorating the social structure of the most important institution ever instated; the institution of family that was laid down by the Great Builder of all things. Drugs had succeeded in taking her from her son, and now she fears that drugs had taken her son from her.

As Margie travelled this long road, the city full of skyscrapers and wonder began to fade, giving way to an even more phenomenal wonder: "nature". The trees reached as high as skyscrapers. She stared at all of this splendor from her seat, and she couldn't help but to let her mind drift and wander...

1983, Margie vs. Crack:
"...She's a super freak, super freak,
She's super freaky..."

The song "Super Freak" by Rick James blared out of the speakers.

Margie was sort of down on her luck and in between jobs. Desperate times called for desperate measures. The one thing about

Margie was that if she didn't have anything, she had beauty. Her worst day was the average chick's best day.

Crack cocaine stimulates key pleasure centers in the brain, causing a euphoric feeling. Crack cocaine is highly addictive psychologically. It pushes people to their own personal extremes.

Margie had reached that point. She didn't want to rob or steal, so she figured she'd try the next worst thing. She had a lesbian friend named Shantaysia. She was the kind of lesbian that looked and occasionally carried herself like a man.

Margie gave her a call. "Hello? Hello, Shantaysia?"

"Yo, Margie! Wassup, fly girl?" How are you?" Shantaysia kicked back in her seat, rubbing her flat top and visualizing Margie's fine form.

In a nervous whisper Margie asked, "You... you remember you said that you and homeboy would look out for me?" She could sense Shantaysia's grin over the phone.

"Well, you know what that entails, right baby?" Shantaysia responded.

"Umm, yes."

Shantaysia's voice was soothing, yet sinister. "It's okay, baby. I'm going to take good care of you in more ways than one. You home now?"

Margie already felt shameful. "Yes," she whispered.

"Alright. I'll be there in like twenty minutes."

Margie sat in her living room contemplating everything in her life. She was feeling an intense anxiety, as though her soul was vibrating too fast for her body.

Her son—her little prince—walked over to her with his eyes

bright like a puppy's. He totally worshiped his mother. In his eyes, she could do no wrong. "Mommy, why do you look so sad?" he asked. He always thought he could help her somehow. He felt like he was supposed to protect her.

"I'm not sad, baby. I'm just thinking about some stuff," Margie responded.

"What stuff?"

"Nothing."

"Mommy!" he said in a very whiny voice.

Margie looked down at her son and squeezed him close to her. "Now Jamaal, everything ain't for everybody to know, *papi*. Some things you got to keep to yourself."

"Are you okay, Mommy?"

Before Margie could respond to Jamaal and his youthful inquisitiveness, there was a knock at the door. "Who is it?" she called out. But she already knew who it was. She felt that deep feeling of guilt and displeasure within herself as she walked with Jamaal to the door and said to him, "I'm fine, baby. Are Fire and the rest of them in front of the building? I'll let you play with them for a little while, and then I'ma come outside and get you. If you need anything, go to Rita's."

Margie opened the door, and standing in the doorway was Shantaysia and Mr. Earl, an older guy that owned an old red moving van. Shantaysia stood there with a Cameo flattop that was dyed light brown on the top. She grinned, exposing one gold cap with a Nefertarie symbol etched into it. She had on a cheap and hollow gaudy Gucci link chain.

Mr. Earl was a tall, creepy older Jamaican man who was always driving his beat up old van and spending his money on young girls.

As the two entered Margie's house, Shantaysia spoke to Jamaal. "Hi, Jamaal. Such a little cutie pie!"

Jamaal was usually friendly to his mother's friends, but these two rubbed him the wrong way. He said nothing in response, and just went outside. His silence spoke volumes. It was a statement of distrust, and rightfully so.

Margie walked her two guests down the hallway to her bedroom with thoughts spinning around and racing through her head. She was psychologically battling with herself and making excuses for her behavior. She told herself, *"I'm just doing it this one time. It's just to get on my feet. I won't do it again."*

However, there was another side of her that told her she was going to a deep, dark and deadly place of no return. And once she sacrifices her particular morals and principals, there is no salvaging such parts of yourself when you have buried your inner child beneath the debris of guilt and sin.

Margie was straightforward about the whole deal. As soon as they got inside her bedroom, before she could take off her clothes, she put her hand out, demanding her two hundred dollars pay.

Mr. Earl dug into his pocket and paid her the money with a devilish look on his face.

Then all parties began to take their clothes off.

Mr. Earl was in awe. Margie was a young woman who he always lusted after and knew that he could never have. For four years straight she had ignored all of his advances—never mind that he was a fifty-three year old man with a tall, lanky wiry frame with big muscles and thick sideburns. But the only thing that really stood out about him was his extra-large hands that seem to imply that he'd been a hardworking man all his life.

Mr. Earl's size thirteen steel toed construction boots seemed to make the loudest noise when he took them off and dropped them on the floor.

Shantaysia took off her velour track suit and stripped down to her BVD's. When she took her underwear off, she had a nine inch rubber strap-on penis dangling from her pelvis. It looked awkward because it was white.

Margie looked like a young frightened damsel in distress as Shantaysia and Mr. Earl watched in awe as she took her clothes off to reveal a body that was only a stretchmark short of pure perfection. Her feet were a perfect size, and her legs were thick and strong, connected to her wide hips and small, slender torso. Her curly locks of hair draped around her chiseled butterscotch features.

Shantaysia and Earl marveled at the sight of the Black Venus. Earl instantly became erect, while Shantaysia's vagina began to drip with moisture and her nipples hardened on her saggy breasts.

Margie accepted the payment, but that did not mean that she would enjoy the ordeal. This was her first time ever having a three-some, and it was her first time in engaging in sex for money.

As she lay on her back on the bed while being groped by two people she felt were most undesirable, every touch made her cringe. Every sensual whisper nauseated her.

Shantaysia began kissing Margie's thighs and said, "I know how to loosen you up." Her soft, sensual kisses began to slowly work up and down Margie's legs.

Margie grabbed Earl's pulsating penis and began to stroke it up and down.

"Now that's the spirit!" uttered a very pleased Earl.

Margie is bearing the entire ordeal, and knows that the better she acts, the quicker Earl will climax and be done with it. So, she went into her woman's grab bag of faking pleasure. She moaned and groaned, and ground her pelvis back and forth. She pulled Shantaysia's face into her vagina and said, "Eat my pussy, motherfucker!"

Then before Earl could even pay attention to Shantaysia's act, Margie looked up at him. "Give me that dick!" she said before she slurped up all nine inches of his dick in one big gulp.

Earl's eyes rolled back. He was in a state of ecstasy. He reached to grab Margie's hair to direct the fellatio, and Margie slapped his hand away, signaling that she was in control and in charge.

What started off as an awkward, offbeat rhythm became a well-tuned symphony of three bodies engaged in an act of lust and debauchery. Even in the midst of all the sinister pleasure, Margie's self-esteem plummeted even deeper as tears began to roll down her face. At first, she felt guilty for committing the act, and now her guilt lay in the fact that it brought her pleasure. She hated herself for honestly enjoying it.

******

Elsewhere, Jamaal abandoned Fire and the local neighborhood kids. He couldn't quite get into the groove of playing freeze tag. Something in his gut said that he should check on his mother. He couldn't shake that itch inside, so he decided to go back home.

Jamaal had a way of leaving the front door to his building and apartment unlocked when he was out front, so he quietly crept into the house. His first intention was to just check on his mother and then run back outside, but the weird sounds of groaning attracted his attention. This was a sound he only heard when his father was around.

As he moved closer and closer to the door, his six year old mind was racing with questions like, *"Why are they making that noise?* And *"Are they hurting Mommy? Are they hurting Mommy?*

******

At this point, the three people in the bedroom had switched positions. Earl was stroking Margie doggie-style and slapping her ass like she was a two dollar whore, while Margie's face was buried between Shantaysia's legs. It was a sexual romp that Caligula himself would have envied. The three moved about in sexual bliss with hearts pounding.

At the point of zenith and epic arousal, the door to the bedroom burst open. "Mommy, are you okay?" Jamaal shouted.

Only Margie heard and saw him first, and their eyes locked.

Jamaal was confused, bewildered and disgusted in that very moment. He was feeling emotions that were too intense to withstand. His young fragile mind scrambled to make logic of it all. "Stop! Stop hurting my Mommy!" he burst out screaming. "Help!" That was all he could do. He didn't know what was going on. He just wanted to erase that moment. He ran out of the apartment.

Margie and Shantaysia quickly got up and got dressed, while Earl's age didn't allow him to move as quickly. No one spoke; there was nothing to speak about.

Margie took off running after 'lil Jamaal.

Earl was left in the apartment, shuffling off like the parasite he was, while Margie wept because she knew it was all wrong.

Margie caught up to her son and held him while he cried, "Help! Help! Help!" But eventually the sound faded.

All Margie could say was, "Sorry, baby!" as she held his little body tightly.

Jamaal's murmurs of "Help!" changed to "Why? Why? Why, Mommy?" He pleaded with her to make him understand what he saw. He could not flat out describe it or define it, but he just knew it felt wrong.

So, to help him understand, Margie looked him deeply in his eyes while holding his face and said, "Babe, you didn't see anything."

"Okay," he responded.

Was it evil to constantly alter lil' Jamaal's reality by getting him to deny the truth? Or, was it a "necessary evil" to shield him. Or, was it teaching him to shield himself?

Jamaal had to deny his pain and repress his emotions to hold onto his sanity. Like magic, it was done, and the moment that he said, "Okay," he erased what had happened and buried it in the deepest corner of his psyche.

But the damage was done. It caused a rift in his relationship with his mother. Protect his mother, he did at twelve. He broke Earl's arm with a baseball bat during an altercation with Margie.

You can lie to everyone except yourself. You can deceive anyone except yourself. But every dark must come to light. Everyone has deeds they wish to keep secret; at the least an impure thought never shared. What happens when we become transparent, and the one thing you wish you could hide is exposed?

******

A bus attendant touched Margie's shoulder ever so lightly and said, "Excuse me, Miss. We've arrived at Lewisburg Penitentiary."

CHAPTER 5

FREEDOM

FREEDOM has been in federal custody for thirteen long years, He did most of his time in Lewisburg Penitentiary, and was scheduled to be released very soon because he had accumulated about 702 days of good behavior. This roughly reduced his sentence of fifteen years to about thirteen years.

Freedom had taken a bullet to the shoulder and passed out next to his wife's bedside, only to awaken in federal custody and at the center of a high profile case. That kept him in and out of federal court an entire year. He was being used as bait for Sopa, who was the "big fish" the feds were trying to fry.

When the feds couldn't get Freedom to snitch on Sopa, their next strategy was to force him to take all the weight for over twenty different hits ordered by Sopa during his reign. Luckily for Freedom he beat the murder charges for lack of evidence. But Freedom had to take a plea for a lesser charge under the RICO Act. He copped out to fifteen years for conspiracy to distribute crack cocaine.

Fifteen years was the best option available considering the fact that the feds had everything from confidential informants to wiretap evidence against him. If he would have taken his case to trial, he would have faced the possibility of doing life in prison, and never getting the chance to see his lovely daughter grow up.

During his time in the penitentiary, Freedom became familiar with other likeminded individuals who enlightened him to different levels of thought. He shared a cell with a brother named Toussaint Michele Baptiste, a Haitian kingpin. Toussaint was a round-headed old man with an abundance of wisdom. He and Freedom became friends over a chess rivalry.

So many things had changed for Freedom during his prison time. It was a chance for him to sit down and evolve mentally and emotionally.

Samaya did her best to visit as much as possible, but even that began to fade. Thirteen years is a long time for a woman to stay completely loyal, even for a woman like her. He still remembers her very last visit...

******

Before Samaya started to fade away from his life, her visits went from once a week to once a month, to hardly at all. She began to ignore his calls, and seemed to never be home anymore. It wasn't the fact that he was gone so long that made her distant. It was the incidents that transpired before he went to prison that left a sour taste in her mouth.

Samaya almost died being loyal to Freedom. Her daughter, Rain could have gotten killed when the Jamaicans shot up her home.

When Samaya recovered from her gunshot wound, she learned from Chyna that Freedom had been cheating on her with Mercedes.

Samaya would stay up late nights and wonder if her relationship with Freedom was worth salvaging.

In her letters to Freedom she begged him to change. But no matter what, time and distance only made her love grow weaker, while his grew stronger. And to top it off, even his daughter, Rain became somewhat distant.

Rain was foreteen years old, and the reality of why her father was locked away began to kick in. You can't raise a child from behind bars, and from the age of seven Rain became accustomed to a new man in her household. Actually, she never had a chance to become accustomed to her own biological father.

As Rain matured, she began to resent her father for his absence. She longed for a normal life where she could see her real father on a regular basis. She went from calling her stepfather "Abdul" to calling him "Dad".

Freedom felt her slipping away when he called the house and Rain seemed more distracted. Their conversations became shorter and shorter until they turned into a simple "Hi" and "Bye".

Samaya finally found what she had wanted: a simple Muslim man who had a decent job. Abdul was a mature older man in his early 40's who worked two jobs. He worked at the post office, and when he wasn't working there he would illegally use his car to drive cab.

As much as Samaya missed Freedom, she enjoyed the stability and peacefulness of a normal life. Her main regret was that Rain didn't have her biological father around.

Freedom had left Samaya with a nice amount of money, but there was no amount of money that could sustain a woman and a growing child for thirteen years.

Supreme was a loyal friend. He provided Samaya and Rain with as much financial help as possible, but she was too proud. She refused to constantly take money from him, and preferred to earn her own living.

******

Freedom's time in the federal penitentiary system was marred by depression and violence. He stressed over the loss of his family. His violent past followed him through each facility. Multiple attempts were made on his life. He was a marked man, and unlike the streets, he had no soldiers to back him up.

However, the Deadly Lion Posse and La Compania had various hitmen throughout the prison system who were anxious to collect the bounty placed on Freedom's head. No one would stand next to him or be affiliated with him for fear of losing their lives, except for two individuals; Toussaint Baptiste a.k.a. Money Mike, and Yusef Arnold a.k.a. Seth.

CHAPTER 6

DEAR MAMA

"...Dear Mama,
Even as a crack fiend, Mama,
Your always a Black Queen, Mama..."

"Dear Mama", By Tupac Shakur

MARGIE got off the bus and stood before Lewisburg Penitentiary. As she got closer and closer, the penitentiary seemed to grow larger and larger, and began to tower over her. The building resembled a medieval castle. To her it was an old, ugly and haunted landmark of slavery. She charged headfirst at the large, brownish-green giant edifice of horrors behind steel cell doors.

It had been years since she and Freedom had seen one another. Freedom had his resentments and some abandonment issues.

The air was so frigid and cold that Margie could see her own breath.

She scanned the area, looking at all the tired visitors. She could see the distress and pain on their faces, but every possible expression was overpowered by one feeling, and that was shame. Visiting anyone in prison is a long, demanding process where for a brief moment you are treated just like an inmate. Visitors are required to walk through a maze of metal detectors. In every corridor there were groups of guards with judgmental looks on their faces.

Margie could not contain her snarl. She rolled her eyes, sucked her teeth and gave off as much attitude as possible.

As she was being led to the visiting area, her mind wandered off to her sacred place in her head where she kept some of her fondest memories. She could still see her black curly haired little boy, Jamaal, running all over their apartment. He was such a busybody. She wondered if he was still sweet; what he looked like now, and had all the years of hardcore street life change him. "*Will he still love me? Will there be any resentment?*" she wondered.

******

Elsewhere in the facility, Freedom sat in his cell, totally oblivious to his pending visit.

Officer McGuire walked the hall. McGuire stood about six feet three inches tall. He was fat and bald, and had bright gray eyes that seemed to blast out beams of pure hatred. He had a deep-rooted hatred for Freedom after overhearing him in the yard "building" with other Five-Percenters.

Officer McGuire banged his baton up against Freedom's bunk and said, "You got a visit. Get out here."

On that particular day, a visit was the last thing that Freedom expected. He could not think of who it was at first, but as he ran down a list of people who would visit him, there was only one person who would do that. It had to be his mother.

As he was led down the corridor by the officer, it seemed like the longest walk.

It had taken years for him to forgive his mother for abandoning him, and then years for him to understand that she really didn't abandon him. She had abandoned herself. She couldn't be there for him.

Freedom and Margie had corresponded via letters and phone calls, but they still hadn't seen one another in a very long time.

Margie was finally at a place where she could play a supporting role in his life. After years of struggling with her addiction, she was finally prepared to be a mother. It may have been too late, but better late than never.

The visiting room was filled with round green plastic tables and chairs, and the brick walls were a light greenish/gray.

Margie felt like an inmate with all the security and metal detectors. The entire process was very degrading. She endured it all for the sake of her son, but also for her own sake. She needed to see him; see how he has grown, and to look into his eyes.

She took a seat at one of the tables and sat there patiently. She had aged so gracefully that you would have thought she was Freedom's girlfriend, not his mother.

When Freedom was brought out, Margie spotted him instantly and shouted, "Jamaal!"

He could feel the love and other mixed emotions. As he walked toward her, his upper lip began to quiver and his knees began to feel weak, as though he would fall flat on his face. He tried his best to restrain his inner child, but tears burst from his eyes.

Margie stood up and grabbed her 6'1" 195 pound son. He melted in this little woman's embrace, and his tears rolled off of his face and inter his mother's hair, as her tears soaked the chest area of his beige jumpsuit.

For a brief moment, everything was okay. It was like he and his precious mother were floating in outer space like two celestial bodies held together by each other's gravity. All the pain was gone.

They say that love is an emotion or a feeling that cannot be easily defined by anyone. Freedom loved Samaya and Rain. He loved Supreme like a brother. He loved Fire, and he even loved his father. But no one could replace the level of affection that he had for his mother. Perhaps it was because their love was formed in adversity. He was forced to think and act like a grown man at an early age.

Their brief moment of peace was abruptly interrupted by the Officer McGuire. "Okay. We don't allow much of that hugging."

Just as quickly, they were both brought back down to the harsh reality that this is not a banquet hall for a family reunion. No, this place was far from that. It was not even state prison; it was a federal penitentiary. It has housed some of the hardest criminals that America has ever seen; people like Al Capone and John Gotti.

Freedom turned around and looked at the officer, but it was okay because Margie grabbed his hand and he sat down across from her. Before she spoke, she examined him from head to toe.

Freedom had grown bigger and stronger. He kept his hair cut low, and she could see his jet-black waves. He allowed his beard to grow out. If you didn't know him, you would assume that he was a Muslim. He was definitely a disciple of some sort, but not a true Muslim.

Margie had heard the rumors and the war stories, and she knew that she was sitting across from a "beast".

Freedom's tears had dried up and his eyes went cold. At that moment, Margie could see into his soul. All she saw in him was a killer.

Freedom examined his mother, and was pleased that she was

thick. Her eyes were clear, and he could tell that she was clean (drug free). Yet he saw her pain and her guilt over the years of negligence.

Margie's lip quivered as she grabbed his hands from across the table and said, "Baby, I'm so sorry!"

"Sorry for what, Mom?" he asked.

"For neglecting you and for not being there when you needed me."

This was Freedom's moment. This was his chance to tell her how fucked up his childhood was. He could tell her how angry he was and that he was hurt when she abandoned him. But instead, he offered her comfort, suppressing his emotions for her sake. "Mom, it's okay. At least you're here now," he said.

"I missed you so much, baby!"

"I missed you too. So, what you been up to?" he asked.

Margie spoke of her struggles getting off drugs. She told him of all the progress she's made in her life.

Freedom told Margie about her first grandchild, Rain.

"So, baby, you know that you have to do things differently now. You've lost about twelve years of your life to this system," Margie said.

Freedom didn't want to hear her preaching, but out of respect he listened, and some of the info actually sank in.

Margie continued. "Baby, I know you don't want to hear this, and you're probably tired of it, but during the last couple of months you got left in here, think about what you're going to do. You've been shot. You could be dead. You could be serving life in prison. You're still young, babe. You have a second chance at life. Don't squander it for fast money."

"Okay, Mom."

"You've always been an intelligent young man, *papi*. You're an old soul with so much to offer this world. Be the person that God meant for you to be."

"I will work on it. Just remember that this was all I've ever known since birth."

"No, it's not, *pa*. You're bigger than that. You're greater than just that. I know I might have led you in the wrong direction, Jamaal," she said with a guilty look on her face. "Can I confess something to you?"

Freedom was immediately intrigued. "Yes, Mom."

"Do you remember that time when you caught me doing some sexual shit?" she asked him.

Freedom's expression sank as his mind traveled back in time to that incident and resurrected some horrible feelings. "Yes. I remember it as a dream or something. You told me that it never happened."

"Well, it did happen."

Freedom's face dropped and he asked, "Umm, Mom, are you serious?"

"Yes, Jamaal."

"So, Mom, after all these years, why did you decide to tell me the truth now?"

"Because I want you to forgive me… well, actually because I want me to forgive me!"

Freedom leaned forward and looked his mother in the eyes while holding her hand. "So, you came all the way over here for redemption? Mom, I forgave you a long time ago. I know that you had your struggles. Life wasn't' easy for you, Mom. But I'm so proud of you!"

"Are you still running around calling yourself God?" she asked.

"Yes and no. Spiritually, I've learned and studied so many things. I can't say that I am God, but I'm definitely part of Him, and He's inside of me."

"Good. So do me a favor and pray. Just pray, and when you come out, change your life. I'll look for a work program and see if I can get you a hook up with a job or something.

The rest of Margie and Freedom's conversation went well, and they laughed and caught up on old times.

Margie left with a sense of satisfaction. She finally got her baby back.

Freedom walked back to his cell pleased that his mother had given him the greatest gift ever by becoming clean and sober.

They had been a dysfunctional family for the first decade and a half of his life. The scars they had accumulated from years of drug abuse and domestic violence on his father's part were healing. They made the first step by instilling hope, faith and love into one another's lives, and reunited once again as mother and son.

The Affair:

Supreme's massive 6'3" 220 pound frame was chiseled to perfection. He stood in front of Mercedes, resembling an African god. His long dreadlocks cascaded down to his shoulders and down his back like a silk waterfall flowing over his chocolate, mountainous trapezius muscles.

All Mercedes could do was lust after him as he began gently kissing her body from head to toe, and sucking and suckling every part of her like she was composed of tender, juicy morsels.

Mercedes was extremely voluptuous, with a tiny waist and huge juicy buttocks that was complimented by thick, muscular legs and delicate feet. She had the type of body that made a man feel like she was born to please.

Their love affair was so wrong, yet so right at the same time. Over the years with Freedom locked away, she formed a relationship with Supreme. He filled a huge void in her life left by Sopa and Freedom being gone.

Mercedes was the ultimate mistress. She still loved Freedom, but she was the type of woman who moved like a man. She would gladly exchange sex for power, and every move she made was strategic.

Supreme was still in love with Chyna, but taming Mercedes was like a challenge for him. She was very well-known in the drug underworld, and to have her came with esteem and prestige. Besides that, she was a professional transporter, or what they call a "mule".

Mercedes looked up at Supreme with a slight hint of shame in her eyes and said, "*Papi*, you know that Freedom will be home soon. I don't think we can keep this up much longer."

"What do you mean by that?" he asked.

"Well, let's be real, *papi*. You and Free are like brothers. I can't come between that. If he finds out, he'll be hurt, and y'all two will never be the same."

Supreme gently grabbed her hands, raised her off the bed and embraced her succulent frame. "Why does he have to know?"

"Because we can't fake it in front of him. And honestly, after all this time, I still love him."

"Love? What do you know about love? People like me and you only love one thing, and that's money."

"No, I actually love Free. Don't you? We never meant to go this far, and I wouldn't want to disrespect him by doing it in his face. That would be foul, you feel me, *papi*?" Mercedes explained.

Supreme looked a little disappointed, but he understood. "So, is this our last time?" he asked.

"Yes, so let's make it count."

He slipped off his clothes, and she rushed to taste his body all over. Their bodies swayed to the groove and gyrated until they had multiple mutual orgasmic explosions.

Kendu:

Kendu swerved down the Van Wyck Expressway in his Mercedes Benz S-Class Jeep with all black leather interior. He was a trip.

He had met Supreme up north in Watertown. He was sort of like Supreme's connection. He just had all the connects.

Kendu had on black Levi's, a black Polo shirt, and was draped in a black mink coat. He was a light-skinned Al B. Sure looking dude. He could drive, sniff coke, drink Hennessey, smoke a cigarette and talk on the phone at the same time. He was a unique brother who had been doing business with Supreme and Lex for a while.

Kendu's real name was Kashif Ali, but his grandmother used to call him Kendu, so he kept the name.

He knows Jamaica, Queens as well. He had a lot of connections and knew where to get anything and everything. He was one of the few guys who could get any drug into the jails.

Kendu had a crazy schizophrenic/bipolar chick named Stacey. Stacey was just as wild as Kendu was. She was the result of an inter-racial couple. Her father was Black and her mother was white. If you saw Stacey, you would have thought that she was Dominican. She had bright gray eyes and golden bronze skin, and sort of a sultry-smooth voice. Carol was cool as shit until she hit her breaking point.

Then it's over. She could be that bitch. She was a sexy gangsta who was definitely perfect for Kendu.

Stacey was also the pill connect. At any given time she could get Xanax, Oxytocin, Seroquel, and other heavyweight stuff, including ecstasy.

Kendu took a quick bump (sniff of coke) when his phone rang. "Yo, who dis?" he asked.

"This is Supreme."

"Peace, God."

"You got that for me?" Supreme asked.

"Yeah, there're twenty-five stacks each," Kendu replied.

"How many you got?"

"Twenty."

"So, give me ten for $200,000."

"Naw. Ten for $220,000."

"Okay, you got it. Oh yeah. We gotta start tightening this ship up. You know Freedom is coming home."

"Say no more." Kendu said and hung up his cell phone. "Everybody keeps talking this Freedom coming home shit, but I don't know who the fuck Freedom is!" he said to himself.

CHAPTER 7

EYE FOR AN EYE

AT Impulse Restaurant located on Guy Brewer Boulevard right off of Jamaica Avenue is some of the best West Indian food in New York City. But if you weren't familiar with the area, you wouldn't know that the restaurant was in the basement of Impulse Salon & Barbershop.

Impulse Salon & Barbershop was in the epicenter of a bustling Black community. It was a place where anybody who was anybody came to get groomed. Plus, you got an update on the lowdown/gossip.

Black Bobby all but owned the barbershop. It made a good front for his weed and coke business. He was a certified O.G. (original gangster). He was a skinny, loud and obnoxious type of guy who was always joking around. It was hard to tell if he was serious or not because he never let you in that far. He was the type of dude who was fifty years old, looked thirty and acted like he was twenty.

Black Bobby was a heavy hitter in South Jamaica, Queens, Bed-Stuy, Brooklyn and the Bronx. He was well connected, and had his hands in all different things like coke, sour and gun running. The only thing he didn't do was cut hair, even though his clippers were just as notorious as his guns. Ironically, both were used to hurt people.

Despite Black's lack of skill in the cosmetology field, his chair was always filled with customers waiting for him. He was lethal and smooth with the transaction process.

Black would make weight sales right under the owner's nose. His method was sweet and simple. His weight customers always came in with clothes in shopping bags. Black always kept sneaker boxes in shopping bags. Depending on the price and the customer, anything could be in that sneaker box. His clients would sit in his chair and get a haircut while placing their orders. All the while, Black would make it good for the crowd by telling random jokes and commenting on the latest rap news. His loud persona was all smoke and mirrors for the magic that was happening right in front of everyone's eyes. This was all an act for making his money. But we'll get back to him in a minute…

******

The architecture of Impulse Salon & Barbershop and Impulse Restaurant was simply an amazing feat in Black entrepreneurship. The owner truly mastered and targeted a specific demographic.

The barbershop is situated next door to a two story beauty salon that is attached to Impulse Restaurant in the basement. It is a bustling business that caters to Jamaica's heavily Caribbean population.

The restaurant in the basement was very busy that particular day. The owner, Donovan—Don for short—was in a meetings all day with multiple business associates in his private office.

Don was a shrewd Haitian man in his 40's. He made a fortune by slicing throats in Little Haiti down in Miami. Since the early 80's he had been laundering his money and funneling it through his restaurant and salon chains throughout the east coast.

Don was the type of cat that actually did things the right way. He made up his mind to retire from the street life and moved to New York and settled down. But his past in Miami was too strong to escape. He kept his street ties, but instead of being a gun for hire, he was more of a connections person. If your name was good with him, then he could connect you to someone else whose name was also good. He would get a little money off the top when the deal was done.

On this particular day Don had two special visitors from Jamaica.

Don was wearing all black, dressed in classy hard bottom shoes and a silk button up shirt. He had a big bulb-like head with a receding hairline, and he kind of had a walk that let you know that he was constantly in the gym.

He glided through his establishment like a politician campaigning, kissing babies and waving hello. No matter how courteous and polite Don was, you could still see something dark in his eyes.

Don had a custom of keeping the music playing in his office just in case his office was bugged or his phone was tapped. The feds didn't stand a chance of hearing past the music, and even if they did, they also had to decipher the thick Haitian accents that flowed in and out of certain dialects.

Don entered his office to find his esteemed guests waiting for him.

The first person sitting off in the corner of the office was Bulla. Bulla sat there with his five-foot long, large clumpy locks tucked into his all black Rasta cap. He was wearing a tight black thermal under his camouflage army blazer, and G-Star Raw denim pants. His

Rastafarian affiliation was obvious. His blazer was decorated with patches featuring Bob Marley, Marcus Garvey, and Haile Selassie.

Bulla was a human oxymoron. On one hand he was a peace loving vegetarian devout to his culture and the overall betterment of Black people.

On the other hand, he was a stoic cutthroat hitman and stickup artist. How can a human being claim to be righteous with so much innocent blood on his hands?

Bulla was a bitter man well into his 50's. His sleep was filled with nightmares of the faceless souls that haunted him. The murder that tortured his thoughts the most was the one he didn't even commit. When his son Fire died, big part of Bulla had died with him. Bulla's misery stemmed from the feeling that his son died trying to prove himself to him.

Bulla had his little brother Magnum with him. Magnum was a trendy gangster. He sported a Mohawk that twisted up into locks at the tips. He was the Yin to Bulla's Yang.

They hadn't been back to New York in a couple of years. They had moved their operation to New Jersey and Miami.

It had been over a decade since Fire's closed casket funeral was held in Brooklyn. Magnum was there that fateful night at the bar on 145th Street and St. Nicholas Avenue. They had lost some good warriors to Freedom's gun.

Freedom, Supreme and Pistola had rushed in and massacred at least eight Deadly Lion Posse members. Out of the eight, four of them were key players, including Fire, Cutty and Star.

Afterwards, the police shut the bar down during their investigation, and the bar never returned to its full capacity.

In that one night Freedom had crippled New York City's drug

market. The DLP's New York branch was split in half with Harlem finished. The only ones left were a couple of strongholds spread throughout Jamaica, Queens and Brooklyn.

Since Fire's murder, everything in the New York City streets has changed. Nations were divided, and DLP didn't have the same power and presence. The game was dominated by small startup groups that were more locally based. The gang culture was lost in the assimilation of second and third generation Jamaicans who became Americanized.

Ironically, as negative as the influx of the New York gang culture was furthering the division of young urban America, it also seemed to bring some together. Bloods and Crips, or the Peoples and Folk Nations in New York just had different allegiances than say gangs in L.A. In New York, most gangs were multiracial as opposed to ethnicity based. Of course a lot of hustlers stuck with their cultural background.

All of this made for a totally new terrain, and if Bulla and Magnum were going to find a means to an end, they had to adapt.

Bulla's power in the street was weakening. He had allowed Freedom to live too long, and with him getting out of the penitentiary soon, that was the perfect time to arrange his death.

Don shook hands with both men, sat down and began the conversation. "So, the infamous Mr. Bulla and Mr. Magnum," he said with a grin. "I never thought we would ever have a business meeting. I would have thought that we would be aiming guns at each other. Oh, brother!" he laughed.

Magnum usually did all the talking. "Dat was da past. A t'ing of de past will stay in de past. Right now, Mr. Don, me have an itch me need fi scratch. So, what can ya do fah me, boss?"

"Do you want me to scratch the entire itch, or do you want me to point to where it is?" Don asked.

"'Nuff soldier tried to murder de bwoy, but we can't touch him. Even in a jail me still can't touch him. De bwoy home, 'nuff soldier from every blood clot where. Furthermore, me take dis one a lickle personal when it come to de bwoy Freedom. It must be me brethren dat deliver de death blow, understand? Bwoy's blood fi run! Him have some bwoy in Jamaica, Queens from the amount of information I get. Dem bwoys out here, brethren."

"You must mean C.M.K. Money Gang, Kitty Gang and PNA. I know them. I've done some business with them before. They're actually right up the block with Supreme and them."

"Ah know, yuh mean business? Dem bwoys I was wit' we and yuh have some type of business wit' dem pussy clot bwoys."

Bulla interrupted. He was not much for words and he hated procrastination. "Listen here. De bwoy Supreme and Freedom like brothers. Dem move like one body. Freedom's de head and Supreme is de heart. Most time yuh fi chop off de head and kill de body. Well, dis time me afta kill the heart, everyt'ing else gwon follow."

"So basically, you not only want to be rid of him, but you want to collapse his infrastructure."

Magnum interjected. "Yeah, exactly. And right now, him built a firm foundation out here in Jamaica, Queens. Trust me, we have soldiers, but de way dis bwoy operates, we afta kill 'em wit' sophisticated t'ing."

"I understand you completely."

Bulla said, "So, if money ya need, money ya get. But just one lickle extra t'ing me wan. Save the bwoys Freedom and Supreme fo' me. Me wan see him face when me send him to see Jah. Most time me kill fo' business. Dis time it personal."

"One last t'ing, Don. Who you loyal to? Because ya know dem bwoys ya have business wit' dem. So don't wan give ya money fo' nuttin, ya understand?" Magnum said.

Bulla and Magnum took a moment to peer deeply into Don's eyes. They had to be sure he wouldn't double cross them.

"My loyalty is with you, Magnum. We've been peers for years now, and you would do it for me. Now, let me ask you one final question. Why would Bulla and Magnum of the mighty Deadly Lion Posse need the assistance of Haitian Don?" Don asked.

"Well, put it dis way. We try to keep DLP low, under the radar. We hot in Queens right now. Plus, ya have more connections. That's why. And Queens is the terrain for the war, so we get a general who's familiar wit' the geography, understand?" Magnum explained.

Don leaned back in his chair and chuckled before he extended his hand to shake Bulla's, then Magnum's hand. While staring into the brothers' eyes he said, "We have a deal. Now, let's eat."

Don's chuckle had a greater story behind it. All three men knew the truth behind why Bulla and Magnum needed him. The Deadly Lion Posse didn't have the same strength in New York as they used to. They had overextended their resources. For the past ten years, everyone they had sent at Freedom was unable to touch him, even in the penitentiary.

Bulla was seeking retribution for his son's death. His passion had evolved into his obsession. Every day that Freedom breathed, Bulla lost more power. He had to not only kill Freedom; he wanted to destroy him. For years Bulla lived with the sorrow of losing his only son, Fire, and he would take any measures to avenge him.

CHAPTER 8

SANGRE DE JESUS

"...Amores dar por complete,
Todo lo que siente alma,
Es entregarse a la vida,
Si es necessario..."

"Amores Como el Nuestro" by Jerry Rivera

AT the Botanica on Arden Street and Broadway in Washington Heights, New York, a beautiful older woman named Maria sat at the counter. Her head was wrapped in white, and she was wearing a white dress and multi-colored beads draped her neck. She wore shades to hide her cataracts while she constantly blew cigar smoke to feed the spirits.

The shelves in the Botanica were adorned with statues of saints like Lazarus and the Virgin Madonna. There were also many different types of candles for multiple spiritual purposes.

Just inside the entrance of the shop was an altar on the floor in the shape of a little gray clay cone, and decorated with cowry shells in the form of a face. This was an altar to Legba, the Guardian of the Gateways. This altar had offerings of money and candy all around it.

At first glance the Botanica seemed to be your typical religious store that you would find throughout New York City and equipped with an elder Santo or Priestess who could give you revelations about your life, a spiritual reading, or a spell for any situation, providing you were willing to pay and you were a believer.

If you were a Dominican from the neighborhood, you would know that it was much more than a typical Botanica. It was one of the biggest cocaine hubs in New York City.

Jose, a young wide-eyed hustler, walked through the door. He was always sure to drop change on the altar as he greeted Maria. "*Hola, Viejita!*"

"*¿Como esta, Chulo?*"

"*Bueno. Bueno,*" Jose said, and gestured to the back of the shop. "*¿Viejito es aqui?*" he asked.

"*Si, mi amor.*"

Jose proceeded to walk to the back of the Botanica and into the bathroom. In the bathroom was a second hidden door with no handle. When he pushed the door open he was smacked in the nose by the most intense smell of traditional Dominican food. There was a platter full of *empanadas* and bowls of *sancocho* and *pulpo*.

Three older men were sitting at a round table playing Dominoes while eating and sipping Brugal. These three men were some of the most dangerous, cold-hearted drug dealers to ever walk the city streets. They belonged to an organized crime syndicate that started in the prisons of the Dominican Republic. This syndicate had a unique hierarchy set up, almost like an exclusive fraternal ordered. It was called "Sangre de Jesus" (The Blood of Jesus).

To outsiders it was thought to be a gang forged on common religious beliefs, and a strict outlook that revolved around Catholicism.

But on the contrary, Sangre de Jesus was the complete opposite. Most of its members were free thinkers who were more into Santeria than Catholicism.

The name of the organization was based on the fact that every member was required to make a blood sacrifice just to be considered for membership. Interestingly enough, the organization only allowed thirteen members at a time, and each member is sworn to secrecy. Their codes, rules and symbolism were all based on numerology, the occult and mysticism.

Collectively, the work is like a criminal congress. Each member is a head of state and generally controls his own operation. Their movements are shrouded in secrecy to the point where some members are considered enemies in the public eye, but comrades behind closed doors. This Machiavellian style of rules and legislature was to serve one purpose. That purpose was power and control. They were firm believers that true power required deception.

The first man sitting at the table and slurping his *sancocho* was Emmanuel, but mostly everyone called him Flaco. He stood about 6"6". He was lanky and had a face full of scars. He always wore shades to hide his soulless eyes, and kept his shoulder-length jet black hair in a ponytail. He was in his 50's, but he dressed like a young man. He wore a navy blue Yankee fitted cap and a Derek Jeter jersey. He would have become a professional baseball player if not for having a big heroin addiction in his younger days. But instead of remaining an addict, he became a supplier. For the past thirty years he'd been moving kilos of *manteca* and has made millions of dollars. Flaco was also known for his itchy trigger finger.

The next man sitting at the table was holding his dominoes in one hand and nursing a bottle of Brugal in the other. He was called

"El Gato" (The Cat). He got his name from being a very stealthy assassin. His appearance was purposely indistinct. Not one for extravagance, he had the gift of invisibility, and was always dressed plain in order to be unnoticed. He was short and slim with narrow squinty eyes and a clean shaven head. He had no facial hair for the sole purpose of being as nondescript as possible.

El Gato was an extortionist. He made a small fortune extorting drug dealers and businessmen alike. He was well-known for his ruthless "anything goes" type of tactics, and was a pure sadist. He had been hired by Colombians and Mafioso's alike. His motto is to never miss a mark.

The third person sitting at the table was an older man in his 50's. He had short gray hair and a receding hairline. He sported a short salt and pepper goatee. His name was Sopa, the notorious leader of La Compania, a cocaine distributing organization that was a lot stronger some years ago, and has since lost its strength.

Sopa was always well-dressed. He loved to wear Tom Ford suits and Ferragamo shoes.

The three men spent the last couple of years putting a stronghold on Sangre de Jesus. They had become the senior members of the group, with another ten members throughout Florida and the Caribbean. Being that they had the Dominican Republic under control and strong ties with the Colombians, this allowed them to get their narcotics at a cheaper and faster rate.

Once Sopa had his connections and his business structure intact, his next move was returning to revive La Compania in New York to restore his northeastern distribution.

In the midst of him rebuilding his empire, his first priority was revenge. He had some old debts to settle. His original plan was to have Freedom murdered in the penitentiary, but that was unsuccessful. So, Sopa decided to come to the United States to do it himself.

Sopa's lieutenant and primary contact in New York was Flaco's little cousin, Jose.

Jose really had no idea what he was dealing with. All he knew was that he was around some real triple O.G.'s. *"Hola, Viejitos!"* Jose greeted when he walked into the room.

"Di me lo, Primo," Flaco responded.

"¿Que fue, Loco?" El Gato said.

"¿Joselito, como esta?" Sopa asked.

"Bueno. ¿Y tu tambien?" Jose asked.

"Sienta te, Loco."

Jose pulled up a chair, and Sopa slid a duffel bag with ten kilos of pure, top of the line Colombian cocaine to him. The cocaine was so pure that even diluted and broken down, you could turn it into about fifteen bricks of coke. On a wholesale level it was worth about $300,000. On a retail level if broken down, the cocaine was worth close to about half a million dollars. This was Sopa's way to jump-start La Compania back into supremacy.

Jose was a master at breaking down cocaine and mixing it with acetone.

"Okay, brothers. Let's get to the matter at hand. As you all know, it is time for us to expand and rebuild our strength in North America. The first place I want is Washington Heights. This is where our people are. If we can't control our people, we can't control anyone else," Sopa said.

"I want you to lean on every dealer there is. If they are not getting their work from us, then they can't exist, period," El Gato added.

"We're taking over New York," Flaco said.

"What about our enemies?" Jose asked.

"Oh, you mean the *cocolo* Jamaican?" Sopa asked.

"Si."

"I've got a special plan for him. That fucking *Moreno* is hard to kill."

"Yeah, from what I hear his crew is out in Jamaica, Queens, and they're strong as hell. He got this guy named Supreme running shit for him until he gets out," Jose said.

"El Gato, that brings me to you. I got a special assignment for you. I need you to take care of something," Sopa said.

"No problema, jefe."

"I got somebody inside of Jamaal's organization, so we'll be able to destroy him from the inside out."

"Pistola will not be a problem. Let me find him. I'll take care of him," Jose said.

"No. I've taught Pistola too well. I don't want you to go up against him. I want Flaco to handle him."

Flaco nodded his head slowly.

"Joselito, I will teach you how to take a pistol apart," Sopa said."

"Sopa, I hear you got a problem with some of them DLP Jamaican *peritos*," Flaco said with a grin on his face.

"No, no. I'm not worried about them. They're weak right now. Their strength is in Jamaica and Miami. They hardly exist out here so I'm not worried about them. Plus, they got problems with the Colombians and the Italian mob. But if we come across a high ranking one, it could get us a favor with the Columbians. Let's keep in mind that our main priority is acquiring wealth. These little motherfuckers we're getting rid of are just speed bumps in the road."

CHAPTER 9

FREE-DOME

FREEDOM spent many sleepless nights in Lewisburg Penitentiary, staring at the walls, crying in silence and missing his daughter. He has spent his 20's to early 30's in the feds.

While the system comes under the guise of reform, the penitentiary only corrupted and hardened his heart. It took time for his mind to adjust to the misery of being secluded behind walls, and years of only experiencing sunlight and fresh air for one hour a day.

Freedom was a strategist, so he spent a great majority of his time making plans.

His cell mate, Money Mike was an old school drug lord. He and Freedom spent hours playing chess. Mike had become a mentor of some sort to Freedom.

Mike was tired of seeing young Black men repeating the cycle of self-destruction and genocide. He knew that the only way to achieve true freedom was to free your mind. He nourished Freedom's interest in the Black revolution.

Freedom was fascinated with the militant leaders of the past, so he researched and studied the likes of Toussaint L'Ouverture, the Haitian liberator; Nat Turner, the freedom fighter; and most of all,

Marcus Garvey. The more Mike taught him, the more he studied and began to truly see the error of his ways.

Freedom wrote Supreme about the knowledge he had accumulated, and suggested that they move onto better things, like cleaning up their money and becoming legal entrepreneurs. But they were living in separate worlds.

Because Freedom's life had slowed down, he was finally able to sit down and cultivate his mind and have a chance to think. His sense of political awareness grew and he began to think of ways to redeem himself and reverse some of the negative energy that he put out there.

As Mike introduced him to more information, his mindset grew. As his historical views and prospects grew, he also became more spiritually enlightened.

He withdrew from the 5-Percenters' teachings and asked himself, "If I am God, then how do I actually become God?" This led him to read the works of authors like Ra Un Nefer Amen's "The Tree of Life", and "The Holy Tablets" by Malachi Z. York. This information he acquired enlightened him to the truth about religion.

Freedom realized that everything originated in Africa, and the Black race is cosmic. There was a great pride instilled in him, and that's when he began to change. He practically begged Mike to give him books and give him more information.

Freedom's selection of reading became broader and delved deeper and deeper, from etymology to theosophy and esoteric astrology. He had blossomed into a scholar, and the only other step for him was to figure out a way to execute all that information. *"What is the point of becoming a scholar without being able to actually manifest the ideas, morals and principles?"* he wondered.

As he evolved mentally, his guilt grew and became a monster that sat on his shoulder. He began to despise the person he had been. He regretted murdering Fire. He was at war with himself. It was his soul vs. his ego.

There is a saying that "God protects babies and fools." At this point, Freedom was neither. *"How could I go on killing my own people? Why couldn't I have figured out a better resolution rather than killing my childhood friend? So much killing; so many Black faces, and I will remember them all, especially Fire's."* He wondered if he could take his new abilities and use them for something positive.

The more he wrote to Supreme about change, the more Supreme resisted. Supreme knew that Freedom was a deep thinker, and labeled Freedom's change as just a jail phase. A lot of folks go to jail and find religion. Few ever leave prison with that religion.

Freedom's biggest dilemma was how to change. The obvious move would be to abandon the entire drug business and take his remaining finances and invest in a legal hustle. That would have been the easy part, except for his enemies. The Dominicans, the Jamaicans and the various victims he had created would not care about his life change. *"How could I become a legal businessman while having to constantly look over my shoulder like a criminal?"*

Freedom came to terms with the fact that he had to settle his debts before anything else. As his relationship with his cell mate Money Mike grew, he shared his inner conflicts and pushed to receive some type of guidance.

Money Mike was a true O.G., and he grew to admire Freedom and looked at him like a son. He decided to help him in every way possible.

In exchange for Mike's help, Freedom would become his face in public.

Mike was a Haitian with international connections due to his mastery of diplomacy, and being a high-ranking 33rd Degree Masonic brother. With an ex-military background, he had connections with the Mob, Zoe Pound down in Miami, judges, lawyers and crooked cops alike.

Mike was also puppet master who could pull strings in the streets from his cell. Just being his cell mate alone gave Freedom access to certain contraband, like a cell phone and the ability to order outside food whenever he felt like it. They even had some liquor in their cell.

Mike needed a protégé; someone to help him manage his business while he served another ten years.

Toussaint was not a king pin in the conventional sense He was more of a catalyst. He connected important people with other important people who wanted to remain unknown. His dirty judges did business with criminals while remaining anonymous. He had acted as a go-between for multiple drug cartels. He also had a lot of people in high places that owed him a lot of favors.

Mike's legal business was being a master tailor. He owned a chain of tailor/dry cleaners throughout Queens and Brooklyn. Mike's tailor shops were his way of laundering his money.

Money Mike was a well-traveled man. His knowledge of the world was abundant due to his travels over fifty years of living. He had been to places like Cairo, Israel and all over Europe, so his views on politics, spirituality and even fashion were worldly views.

As time grew close for Freedom's release, Mike decided that it was time to get him prepared for the world.

Freedom had two months left of his sentence on this particular day, and Mike was on a winning streak beating Freedom six games in a row. Mike cornered Freedom's king and shouted, "Checkmate!" Then looked over at Freedom and asked, "What is the problem with you, nephew? You're not your usual self. You appear to be in a state of melancholy."

"Nah. I just got a lot on my mind," Freedom responded.

"A lot like what? Share your thoughts."

"I know what I want to do. I have a business idea."

Mike rubbed his hands together and leaned forward, eager to hear Freedom's idea. "So, shoot. Let's hear it," he said.

"Okay. I have three ideas. The first one is real estate. Through my studies, I realize that the only thing that truly appreciates and is proven to rise in value as time passes is property. I want to own land. I want real tangible power. I have enough cash to outright buy it, and I want to get into the hustle of flipping houses, feel me? Now, that's my first priority. Oh yeah. I'm working on a self-help book. I just didn't title it."

"My third concept is to have a T-shirt company," he said with a grin.

Mike looked at him like he was crazy. "T-shirts? Are you serious, man? What made you come up with that idea?" he asked.

"Why? Do you think it's a bad idea?"

"Actually, I think it's a great idea. You just never struck me as a fashionista," Mike said and giggled.

"Well, it's not about fashion as much as it's about making a social statement. I want to use the T-shirts to put out a message."

"Okay, I like that. Sounds interesting. So, what are you going to call it?"

"'Necessary Evil T's. It'll be a T-shirt line with a message. I'll use the T's to express certain spiritual, political and social views. See, the phrase comes from the fact that 'necessary evil' in itself is defined as something unpleasant that must be accepted in order to achieve a particular result. It represents us. We are the ultimate necessary evil. Society shuns us, pushes us to the side, yet profits off of our ignorance. We make the fashions, but we are not allowed to profit off of the same styles we make popular. We live in a capitalist society that profits from the pain of poor minorities, yet poor minorities are the major consumers. We buy all the sneakers. We are the biggest consumers and the smallest producers."

Mike was a stocky older man with round features, a shiny bald head and jet black skin. He had wide, soul piercing eyes, and when he grinned, his bright white perfect teeth seemed to gleam. For some reason he put on his bright smile and began to nod his head. He was pleased to see that all those books, chess games and long talks seemed to sink into Freedom's head.

Freedom seemed perplexed. "What? What? Why are you looking at me like that, man?" he asked.

"I'm proud of you. I've watched you develop into a truly intelligent young man."

"Thanks, Mike, but I got a couple of things I'm going to have to figure out before I go completely legit."

"Oh, yes, I'm glad you said that. You're right, and I can help you. First, let me tell you that your enemies have returned to New York, and they are waiting for you to be released."

"What the fuck do you mean?"

"When I learned about all the money you had on your head, I made it my business to research your rivals. Trust me; I've got eyes and ears everywhere."

"Okay, Uncle, so exactly what am I dealing with?"

"Well, that older guy, Sopa is in Manhattan, and from what my sources say, he's out there in New York looking to do more than just kill you. He's come to take over New York's cocaine distrubution."

Freedom nodded his head with a concerned look on his face.

Mike's eyes opened wide as he looked directly into Freedom's and asked, "Have you ever heard of an organization called Sangre de Jesus?"

"No."

"Well, your friend Sopa has risen through the ranks while you were in here. He's basically two times stronger than when you first met him."

"Fuck him! I don't give a fuck! I'm still going to find him and put a motherfucking slug in his head! I can't believe that bastard is still alive anyway! I got to hurry up and get back to the streets!"

"Listen to me, Nephew. You are in a very precarious position right now. This is not the time to lose your head. You know that cooler heads prevail. There is nothing else you can do right now except plan and prepare."

Freedom knocked the chess set over and jumped up in anger.

Mike ironically remained calm and unaffected like a patient adult watching his child having a temper tantrum. Then he continued to speak in a calm, monotone voice. "Yong man, I want you to hear me very clearly. I know that you're frustrated, but people wanting you dead will never stop. You will never have a shortage of enemies, and I got your back. Trust me, if I didn't, I would've stuck a shank in your neck while you slept and collected an easy fifty grand a long time ago. Now, please sit the fuck down and let's figure this shit out!"

Freedom turned around and gave Mike a long hard stare, to

search for any sign of betrayal. But in his gut he could find none. Technically, if Mike was going to betray him, he would have already killed him; not give him vital information. So Freedom sat back down but kept one thing in mind; he can't necessarily trust anyone.

"Now listen," Mike continued. "It gets deeper, because apparently you've got some DLP dudes after you too, but you already knew that. What you probably don't know is that those Jamaican motherfuckers are in New York too. It's like everyone wants to give you a 'welcome home party,' huh?"

"Okay, it's a war. I've got to get rid of those motherfuckers once and for all," Freedom said.

"I can help you with that."

"Nah, I got my own soldiers and connects. I'll call Supreme and Pistola and give them a heads-up."

"Maybe it would be more strategic to come at them from a different angle, because I'm positive that they're assessing your strength as we speak. I'm the one ally that they probably don't know about. I'm your wild card. You might want to use that to your advantage. I also got someone to help clean up your money, but I'll introduce y'all later."

"Cool. Right now, I just need a moment to think," Freedom said.

There is a line in the famous work of Shakespeare's "Henry the IV", and it reads: *"Heavy is the head that wears a crown."* In other words, the problems of a king differ from the problems of a pauper.

Freedom had raised himself to the level of a king, and now his crown was at stake. Inside, he wished that he could disappear and be free of all the conflict and confusion. It seemed like the only good thing he had in his life was the fact that his mother actually reformed herself.

Freedom was once again at a crossroads. His newly found spiritual enlightenment was in direct conflict with his past. He could not move forward to clean up his life and still have the ghosts from his past haunting his every move. *What is a man to do? You can't serve two masters. How can a child of God do the devil's work and remain sane?*

Freedom had told his mother that he would change. He even thought that he'd be able to have Samaya and his daughter in his life once he proved to be a changed man.

The first law of self-preservation is survival. Somewhere in the dark corners of his mind he must have thought that more than a decade in prison would make his bloodthirsty enemies forget him and move on to other endeavors. But instead, his time away gave his enemies time to evolve into his nemeses. Their strengths evolved and grew, and now a pack of bloodthirsty wolves were salivating, scratching and pawing at his door. His mind had to be set. He only had a couple of weeks to truly prepare, because he was not going home to a loving family. He was going home to an army, and he had to be prepared to lead them to victory. It was war!

CHAPTER 10

BIALA DE LA MUERTE

"...The time of the rule of the wicked is up! Whatever God says though shalt not do, the white man says, 'Go ahead!' he is an enemy of divine law! But you Black men and Black women, your nature is obedience to the will of God. But circumstance has made you other than yourselves...!"

THE powerful words of the Honorable Minister Louis Farrakhan rang out loud from the speakers on the first floor of 118-20 Farmers Boulevard.

Samaya and Abdul were home and waiting for Rain to return from school. From her window, Samaya could watch as she got off the Q3 bus.

Playing Farrakhan's speeches were Samaya's way of keeping her home filled with positive energy, and even though she didn't deny Rain her own choices of entertainment, she still made it her business to counteract the barrage of music from the likes of Nicky Minaj and Lil Wayne, and the negative influences of the media and society. It was a constant battle for the mind and psyche of her child, and she was determined to save her from the fate of her father. She also made sure to create balance in Rain's life, and saw to it that Rain read about powerful Black women like Assata Shakur and Queen Tiye.

******

El Gato sat low behind the tinted window of a raggedy old gray Honda Accord. He screwed a silencer onto his 9-mm black Smith & Wesson, and sheathed his heavy, bone-splitting machete into its leather scabbard. "Carmina Burana", a haunting symphony composed by Carl Orff played in the background. El Gato's narrow lips seemed to mimic every tone in the orchestra.

It was all too surreal for Gato. This was just another hit; another murder; another victim, a favor for a favor.

Gato knew as well as Sopa did that every man is different. That's why any group of men that chose to complete a specific task must organize and distribute job functions. Gato's job was to do the dirtiest of dirty work, and he had the stomach for it. He did everything quietly. He hated noise and struggle.

He got out of the car wearing a gray turtleneck, black leather blazer and black fitted jeans. Everything about him looked inconspicuous, and he blended into the community. He was cautious to make sure no one was directly watching him walk towards Samaya's door. When he reached the door, he gently rang the doorbell twice while he listened for footsteps inside.

As Samaya walked towards the door she yelled out, "Rain? Why are you home so early?"

Gato grinned, anticipating an easy kill. As Samaya's footsteps came closer to the door, he stood there silently and practically stilling his breathing while he pulled his bun out of his blazer.

Samaya had been long removed from her days in Harlem. The instincts that she had when she was with Freedom had become atrophied through lack of use. With Freedom, being alert and on guard was a daily routine. She had spent the past decade free of the mindset that comes with being a "hustler's wife". Abdul had offered her a more stable and calm lifestyle. They were a normal middleclass family.

"Rain?" Samaya asked again and paused at the front door.

Usually Rain would answer her mother through the door. Some sort of intuition kicked in. Samaya had to make a split second decision.

"Knock, knock, knock!"

By the third knock Gato shot the door locks open and rammed the door with his shoulder.

Samaya quickly turned around and darted into her kitchen.

"Samaya?" Abdul yelled, charging into the kitchen.

Abdul was 190 pounds of muscle. He was a 6'2" Muslim brother with a very full beard. He was like a giant compared to Gato. But like David slew Goliath with a stone, Gato slew Abdul with a slug.

Simply responding to all the noise, Abdul was caught off guard, and the first shot caught him in his neck, causing him to stumble and fall backwards.

Gato was relentless. Not wasting any time, he ran over to Abdul's body and stood over him with a grin while Abdul begged and pleaded, "Why are you doing this? I have a family!"

Gato replied with a grin before putting two more bullets into Abdul's face, "It's just business."

Even with his skull cracked open and nearly obliterated, Abdul's body still twitched.

Samaya lunged at Gato with a butcher knife and cut him on his wrist which caused him to drop his gun.

"Aye coño, puta!" he screamed, and answered her assault swiftly

and deadly. A left hook to her ribs sent her careening against the counter, and she flopped to the floor.

Samaya was filled with rage. She had a feisty spirit, but was overwhelmed by Gato's brute force. He pounded on her, kicked and stomped the beautiful defenseless woman, and finally choked her with all his strength.

Samaya fought back fiercely, trying to remove the vise grip chokehold from her neck. Tears flooded her eyes as she felt her life slipping away. Her eyes were bloodshot red, and felt as though they were going to pop out of her skull. Thoughts and memories of Freedom, her mother, childbirth, her husband and her daughter Rain flickered like flashes in her mind. In one final act of defiance, she reached out and scratched Gato's face deeply and slowly.

Gato just squeezed her neck even tighter until a final breath oozed out of her body. Her eyes were frozen and focused with a mixture of rage and fear swirling throughout before the final spark faded.

Gato was not fazed at all, but simply aggravated with his own poor performance. He should have been able to enter, do the hit and leave smoothly. He couldn't believe this woman almost stopped his business. He retrieved his gun, unsheathed his machete and got to work.

Anyone could have pulled the hit off, but Gato was not just anyone. He was different. He was the type of hitman that's used to make a statement. When you wanted to send a horrific message throughout the underworld, he was the perfect hitman. In fact, he was no mere hitman; he was a squalid sociopath with an acute proclivity for violence.

Gato was a surgeon with his machete. He began by removing

Samaya's limbs one at a time beginning with her ankles, then her knees, all the while humming his favorite opera. He was a mad sadist and regretted not having enough time to keep her alive while he swiftly eviscerated her vagina.

After Gato completed his masterpiece, he stepped out of the house, quickly jumped into his car and sped off. Speeding up the block, he swerved, just barely missing a pretty young girl.

That pretty young girl was Rain. She was frozen like a deer caught in the headlights. She couldn't react quickly enough to move out of the way, and breathed a sigh of relief when the car swerved and avoided her. "Thank God that car missed me! If I got hit, Mom would beat my ass!" she said to herself.

Rain was an intelligent, beautiful little girl whose life was sheltered. She knew about her father's history, and she resented him. At the age of fourteen she hadn't seen her father outside of prison for twelve years. She hated taking the long trips to see him behind a wall. She still loved him, but she had entered her teen years. She had emotions that were an amalgamation of puberty and frustration. It would take time for her to understand her father's "necessary evils".

Rain walked up Farmers Boulevard to her home with joy in her heart. She was the best of Samaya and Freedom. She had her father's mind and her mother's heart. She had a womanly beauty like her mother, her father's wooly black hair, and both of their almond brown skin complexions combined. She was tall for her age so she definitely stood out while keeping a certain innocence. If she hadn't been known as Freedom's daughter, she would have been harassed more by guys. She was an artist of a sort and loved to paint and draw to express herself.

The self-professed "nerd with swag" knocked on her door while simultaneously ringing the bell with her other hand. But when she knocked, the door swung open slowly, revealing a hideous tragedy. She was the first person to gaze upon the massacre. Those images were repulsive and demoralizing.

Gato had spread her mother's intestines all over the kitchen, and pieces of her body had been flung all over. Her limbs were scattered all around.

Rain's eyes opened wide while her mind screamed, *"Close your eyes!"* But she couldn't; she

couldn't let go. It had to be a sick nightmare; an orchestra of slaughter. Her eyes welled up with tears and her mind shouted, *"Scream!"* But she couldn't do that either. She was stifled with shock.

Choking on every word she whispered, "Mommy! Mommy! Mommy!" Leaning over her mother's limbless torso and trembling in fear, her eyes scanned the room. She soaked in every retched detail, forever defiling her once unsullied soul.

Rain's cerebral fortitude was collapsing like shattered glass. She had to grow up all in that moment. Her heart was heavy. She had lost everything. Her mother, the only guidance she ever knew, was gone. The atrocities and depth of violence that at worst would elude most people's perceptions were now embedded in her psyche, and altering her mindset forever.

CHAPTER 11

BUILD AND DESTROY

SUPREME swerved through traffic in his all black and black leather interior 2010 Infiniti I35. It was one of his many cars. He was en route to do some "maintenance" at one of his Jamaica Avenue territories. He had figured a way to execute a plan that he and Freedom created, but it would take him, Kendu, Pistola and Elmo to execute the idea.

All over Jamaica Avenue in every little pocket there were tattoo shops, little boutiques that sold authentic and fake designer clothing, CD's stores that sold bootleg mix tapes by Superstar Jay, DJ Envy, Kay Slay and many other great DJ's of that era.

The Avenue was prime real estate for the unified hustle era. Black organized crime seemed to disappear in the new millennia. It seemed like rappers like 50-Cent and the LOX's represented the old Black gangster energy.

The streets were harder to organize for an O.G. Men no longer rallied behind leaders. Instead they rallied behind dollars and fads. And with the evolution of computers, every phone came with a camera, and surveillance is at an all-time high after September 11th. Long gone are the days of honor, morals and nobility. Snitching was the new trend, so the purebred had to move shiftier.

Supreme knew that with all the drugs he and Kendu were moving, they had to form a front. Plus, Freedom was constantly writing him about going legit.

Out of respect, Supreme still listened to Freedom. He rented out a couple of small tattoo shops, boutiques, and bootleg CD/DVD shops all up and down Jamaica Avenue and filtered their drug money through those shops.

There were two locations he frequented the most that he owned. One of them was a small store in Gertz Mall, and the other was in the Coliseum Mall. He sold a lot of original Black owned clothing lines. Basically, if you were up and coming, he would help you out.

The clothing and tattoo shops made money, creating a great front for the much bigger drug operation.

But, with the money and the power came some powerful enemies. John, a demon of an older man, was the worst kind of adversary. The old Jew simply brought down the property value on Jamaica Avenue with all of his cheap looking discount stores filled with bootleg Jordan's and fake True Religion jeans. It was at a point where when you walked down the Avenue, you thought everything was fake.

"Air Jordan's! Nike's! Timberland's! Step right inside! Tattoos! Designer clothing! Air Jordan's, only $50.00!" Those words blared loudly out of almost every other speaker on Jamaica Avenue.

John worked with the DEA and put bulls eyes on the backs of any hustlers he considered competition. He was known for under-paying his employees and disrespecting them at the drop of a dime. He hired and fired thugs with no remorse at all.

Supreme had an uneasy alliance with this exploiter of his Black community.

Then there was Cali. He was a tattoo shop owner who came from California. He was one of those mulatto/Black/Tongan/Pilipino looking dudes, and was a well-respected ally of Supreme. He came to New York and started out handing out flyers, and in five short years he was a boss and an owner. For that reason alone Supreme had to respect him. Cali was also responsible for teaching Supreme about the tattoo game, and all the little nuances of the business.

"So, it's broad daylight, man, and there are too many mother-fucking cameras out here," Supreme said to Kendu, who was sitting in the passenger seat. Elmo was sitting in the back.

"We gotta do something. We can't just let those Jamaican niggas talk shit," Kendu said.

Elmo cocked his Glock back and said, "Just let me handle them niggas."

"No, God. It's not that serious. Why the fuck do you got a gun in my car anyway? I told you, no guns, no drugs, and no liquor, nothing in my car!" Supreme barked.

"I got you, O.G. If the pigs pull us over, I can hold my weight. Plus, I'd rather be caught with it than without it."

Kendu said, "I told you this little muthafucka was a fucking hot head. Who is this Jamaican dude anyway?" he asked.

"The nigga's name is Piggie," Supreme informed him.

Elmo laughed out loud.

Supreme continued. "Yeah, anyway, this dude thinks he's a tough guy. He's been harassing motherfuckers in front of my CD shop."

"Which spot? The one where you got that sexy African bitch working in?" Kendu asked.

"Yeah. Amina keeps calling me and telling me that the nigga

won't stop smoking weed in front of the spot. And, he's running into the CD shop to make his sales too. The motherfucker's acting like my store is his fucking cover. I got some work in there and I don't need this motherfucker making it hot," Supreme replied.

"So, what we gonna do to the nigga?" Elmo asked.

"We ain't doing shit. I'm gonna have a little talk with the brother."

Supreme had learned from Freedom the vital lesson that too much violence was bad for business. He didn't fear the Jamaicans, but he was wary of causing any friction. The Jamaican cliques were well known in Queens, and for years Supreme was able to stay below their radar. He was still just as vicious as he was in his younger years, but he just didn't want to kill anyone over anything trivial.

Piggie was somewhat of a scavenger, not much of a real drug dealer. He played 165th Street between Jamaica and 89th Avenues, walking back and forth, slipping in and out of different store fronts and scouring for coke and weed sales. A self-proclaimed enforcer, he and Soulja were two of the last men standing on 165th Street.

There had been a long history of power struggles between the Jamaicans and Black Americans warring for money, power and respect. But that was in the 90's.

In this new millennium, as the world evolved and became more diverse, so did the ghetto. Now besides the Jamaicans and the Black Americans, second generation Africans have become a major factor in the battle for supremacy on the New York City streets. Unlike a lot of other minorities, Africans usually came from a background where they had some money and they had unity, which is something that African Americans lost a long time ago.

Supreme knew that the Africans were watching him. They owned numerous stores, and they were building an empire throughout the city. Most of their parents were legitimate business owners, cab drivers and shop owners. Up and down 116th Street in Harlem they developed their own bustling community where they practiced group economics. Many of them would travel back and forth to Queens where they established a stronghold of cab drivers, tailor shops and CD stores.

It was a silent rivalry, but Supreme knew that he was being watched, especially by African Biggie who happened to be a high ranking Blood gang member, and had his hand in everything from bootleg movies and clothes to E pills, molly and weed.

"Listen. After I talk to this nigga, I'ma bounce and go see my bitch real quick. Are y'all are gonna need me to drop y'all back to the 'hood, or are y'all staying on the Ave?" Supreme asked.

"I'm staying. I'll just walk to my crib on Hillside," Elmo said.

Supreme proceeded to park upstairs on the Coliseum Mall parking lot.

The three men got out of the car and walked down 165th Street, scanning for Piggie.

When Supreme hit the strip, all eyes were immediately on him. He had an audience.

It was a hot summer day, and Rick Ross' song, "BMF" was very popular. It blasted from multiple CD stores and clashed with tunes from dance hall artists like Vybz Kartel and Movado.

Supreme always wore loud colors, and his Robin jeans seemed to sparkle in the sunlight as they draped over his new Jordan's. His presence was a massive 215 pounds of muscle standing at 6"3'. His long waist-length dreads swung freely. He was an urban king whose crown was a Yankee fitted.

Kendu moved with an old school persona. Like an old time

gangster, he wore a straw hat and $500 Bally shoes. He was the type who couldn't walk or talk without a cigarette hanging from his lips.

Elmo was always in shooter mode, so he walked a couple of paces behind his two older counterparts. He was a skinny, fast and shifty magician of some sort. His pants were always well below his butt, and somehow he could still camouflage his firearm.

Supreme made eye contact with Biggie, who stood on the opposite side of the street with Tyson, a well-known Guyanese enforcer.

Tyson was known for being security for everyone, from well-known rappers to your favorite Reggae artist. Word was that you couldn't come to Jamaica, Queens and shine without Tyson's permission.

Tyson was just as ugly as he was mean. He kept a scowl on his face. He wore the best designer clothes that never seemed to look right on his obese potbelly.

There was always serious tension between Tyson and Supreme, but they had a mutual respect for one another.

Also, Biggie was an ambassador of sorts. He had a unique style, wearing a pair of foam deposit Nike's with a matching dashiki. He was big and black, standing there eating a plate of roasted lamb and couscous while Tyson took long pulls of sour diesel marijuana that seemed to permeate through the entire block.

Supreme and Kendu raised a hand and waved, and Biggie in turn answered with a head nod while Elmo lurked in the background unnoticed.

Tyson said nothing, nor did Supreme, but each man uttered an insult like, "Bitch ass nigga!" under their breath.

Anybody who was anybody was out on the block. It was the perfect time to set an example.

Just when Supreme thought for a second that he might have

missed Piggie, he came gallivanting out of a beauty salon behind a customer.

"Psst! Miss! Miss! Babe! Love! Aye, gyal! Yuh nah hear me?" Piggie was saying to the woman.

"Yo, Piggie! Come here, son!" Supreme yelled over to him.

Piggie walked over to Supreme with a confident look on his face, as though he had no fear, while Kendu stood back to watch for any of Piggie's cohorts. You never knew who might be around. Never underestimate your opponent.

Supreme then addressed Piggie. "Listen, fam. I don't care what you do on this block, but when it comes to any businesses of mine, I don't want you standing by my shit, in front of my shit, and nowhere near my shit!"

"Aye, bwoy, me nah have time fo' fuckery. Nah, bwoy, wha ya chat 'bout?"

Amina, Supreme's worker, stepped outside when she heard the commotion.

"I don't even want to hear all that Jamaican shit, pussy!"

Tempers were flaring.

"Say wah? Pussy, fuck you, nigga! I never been in front of yuh store! Furthermore, dis *my* block! I'm de enforcer who run dis place!" Piggie shouted. He was too confident—arrogant in fact.

Supreme was ready to put his hands on him until he noticed a cop car slowly rolling down the street.

Both men lowered their voices.

Amina nodded her head to indicate that yes, Piggie was a problem.

"Dread, I can't have you making my place hot with all the bullshit, feel me?" Supreme said to Piggie.

"Pussy, suck yah mudda! Ya can't intimidate me!" Piggie shot back.

Supreme stared long and hard at him and waved a finger to warn him as the police car turned onto 89th Avenue.

Supreme moved backwards with a menacing look on his face, as though to say, "Okay, I'ma get you later."

Suddenly, Elmo appeared out of nowhere like a phantom and said, "Don't you ever talk to 'Preme like that!" As the words left his mouth, he swung a wide haymaker, bringing his black Glock down across the bridge of Piggie's nose.

Piggie's face was a lot lighter in color than his body from years of washing it with bleaching soap. His sensitive skin spewed blood, and as he instinctively covered his face and began to retreat, Elmo proceeded to hit him two more times in the back of his head. Piggie ran away at top speed.

Supreme shook his head in aggravation, but Elmo turned to him and just shrugged his shoulders. "Why the fuck did you do that?" Supreme asked him.

"Because I didn't feel the way he was talking to you. We got all these bitch ass niggas watching, so I had to make an example out of him."

Kendu chimed in, "Elmo, get low! Get low, nigga!"

Elmo quickly tucked his gun away and walked off. He dipped into the Coliseum Mall through the 165th Street entrance, and then exited the mall on the 164th Street side and disappeared like a thief in the night.

Kendu lit up a cigarette, and he and Supreme casually walked away while onlookers watched them.

They were gangsters; not the new age gangsters either. They

were old school and chose to abide by the old rules. Their mere presence was a threat to every so called boss on Jamaica Avenue. They had enemies and were feared, but what is worse is that because of the fear they inspired, their enemies were silent. They were hiding in the mire like slithering serpents, waiting for the moment to strike.

Like Freedom always preached: *"There can be no sign of weakness. Weakness is a cancer that can afflict the entire body and mind."*

CHAPTER 12

JEZEBEL

SUPREME swerved through traffic on the Grand Central Parkway, making his way to Midtown Manhattan.

Mercedes was his personal addiction. Their lust had turned into love. Every interaction was an emotional smorgasbord of guilt and passion. He didn't know why she summoned him; all he knew was that he had to answer. He had to see her. He was addicted to her supple voluptuous curves and her soft, wet juicy lips. His lust became an obsession. Like a moth to a flame, he was drawn to her.

Yet he still loved Chyna. He did not want to lose her or leave her. Only there were things he could do with Mercedes that he just couldn't do with Chyna.

Mercedes was a freak. She didn't mind being abused. She loved to get choked while she had her orgasms. She loved to explore sexually, and was completely uninhibited.

Chyna was the love of his life. She was the woman he gave his virginity to. To him, she was an object of purity. It wasn't that she wouldn't do the things that Mercedes did; it's just that he couldn't ever see her that way. To him their relationship was sacrosanct, and a deep, dark secluded place in his psyche was reserved for purity. As nothing in his life was clean, at least Chyna represented the one thing he didn't violate.

He shrugged off his guilt for betraying Freedom's trust. He made excuses for himself and wrote her off as just another one of Freedom's side chicks, even though everyone knew that she was much more to him.

Samaya had left Freedom. Mercedes was one of the last things left, and Supreme had taken that from him. There was a dark cloud over their union, and that cloud was a sign of impending doom. There was a storm brewing. The lightning, thunder and rain was bound to fall.

******

"...And you can see my heart beating,
You can see it through my chest.
'I'm terrified, but I'm not leaving.
I know that I must pass this test.
So, just pull the trigger..."

"Russian Roulette" by Rihanna played in the background as Mercedes opened the door.

Supreme stood there ready to devour her, but first he looked down at his cell phone. He had twenty missed calls from Chyna, and frowned with self-condemnation. Then he turned his phone off and raised his eyes from his phone.

Mercedes placed her hands gently on his chiseled face and slowly moved them from his face to his neck, and then gently caressed his chest.

He uttered, "But the last time we spoke——"

Mercedes placed her fingers over his mouth and said, "Shh, *papi!* Relax!" Then she lifted his shirt, slowly got down on her knees and unbuckled his pants while Supreme closed the door behind him. She took all nine inches of his rod into her mouth, gulping and slurping as though it was her last meal.

Supreme leaned his head back against the door and his eyes rolled to the back of his head. He moaned in submission while kicking off his Jordan's and pulling his legs out of his jeans.

Mercedes was the ultimate seductress, enchanting his mind, body and soul. He had an extreme cupidity for intense sexual intercourse. Her expertise in performing the act of fellatio had him completely sedated.

In the midst of gyrating his hips, Supreme grabbed her hair and aggressively pushed his pulsating penis deeper into her mouth. He was in a state of absolute bliss until an eerie feeling came over him as he gazed at the hall closet. His instincts began to tingle while his thoughts raced at top speed. Something told him that there was someone hiding in that closet. The door was slightly ajar. In between grunts and moans, he nonchalantly peered in the direction of the closet. He was spooked.

Suddenly he noticed a slight glimmer in the darkness of the closet, and was certain that there was someone inside. He didn't want to let Mercedes know that he knew about the potential assassin. He was vulnerable. His pants were down, and he had no gun or weapon to protect himself.

"Why would Mercedes do this to me? Why would she wait all these years to betray me? Who was setting me up? Was it Freedom? The Jamaicans? Or La Compania?" he wondered. *No, it couldn't be Freedom. He wouldn't have me killed over a female.*

It was a task to think and strategize while continuing to act like he was enjoying the oral massage he was getting. There was no time for planning or preparation. He had to move fast because whoever was in the closet had an advantage that could cost him is life.

Supreme calmly let go of Mercedes' hair and looked down at her in adoration. "Mercedes," he said.

She leaned away from his penis just long enough to respond. "Yes, *papi*?"

"Do you really love me?"

"Of course I do."

"Then why the fuck are you trying to set me up!" he shouted while smacking her with all his strength and swiftly grabbing her body and lifting her in a bear hug.

Flaco stepped out of the closet with his gun drawn and pointed at Supreme.

"Don't move, motherfucker, or I'll snap this bitch's neck, ya hear me?" Supreme shouted. Sweat trickled down his face. He didn't recognize Flaco, but he knew that he was definitely La Compania.

Mercedes struggled to break free, but to no avail.

Flaco hesitated. He didn't want to shoot Mercedes, but hesitation can lead to his demise, so he fired his weapon.

In the midst of all the shooting slugs, Supreme swiftly pushed Mercedes' body in the hitman's direction. Ducking low, he swung the door open as Mercedes took two shots to her chest, killing her instantly. Her body flip-flopped around like a fish out of water, bouncing off the wall and leaving a streak of blood as she slid to the hard wood floor.

She was finally free. It wasn't because she had any loyalty to Sopa that she set Supreme up; it was her loyalty to Freedom. It was a way to ease her sins, and a way to free herself from the emotional burden of loving two men whom she could never completely have.

Supreme ran at top speed down the steps as bullets whistled by his ears. Flaco was on his tail, but he was not fast enough.

Supreme made it to his car, and realized that he left his car keys in his pants. He looked down in frustration, finally noticing that all he had on was a T-shirt and a pair of boxers.

His next thought was the police. Surely a barefooted, 6"3' muscular Black man wearing just boxer shorts and a T-shirt in the middle of Midtown Manhattan would definitely attract the attention of the police, so he quickly tried to hail a cab. It took a while because based on his appearance, many cabbies were reluctant to stop.

Flaco had stopped chasing him. He didn't want to cause any more loud commotions than he already had.

Luckily for Supreme, a cab driven by a good spirited African man stopped, and in his strong African accent he asked, "What happened, my brother? Are you okay?"

"No, I'm not okay. I've been robbed. Take me home. I have money there."

The driver let him in and asked, "Where you going?"

"Two-O-Eight Sea Girt Avenue, Far Rockaway,"

"That'll be fifty dollars!"

"No problem, brother. I'ma give you $100 when we get there. You just saved my life."

With his heart racing, Supreme sat in the back of the cab. All he could think about was Mercedes. He looked down at his shirt and saw her blood. The gunman's face was a focal point in his mind. Mercedes must have been shot in the midst of all the commotion.

He didn't worry about his car because it wasn't in his name. There was no evidence of him being there except for his pants and his Boost Mobile prepaid phone in the pocket.

As he pieced things together in his mind, one face seemed to echo in the passageways of his thoughts: *It was Sopa... Sopa... Sopa...* Sopa was back, and they were at war.

Supreme was trying to change. He considered himself a boss. He did not care to be an enforcer anymore, but current events had reawakened a slumbering beast and reinvigorating his propensity for bloodshed.

CHAPTER 13

TEMPEST OF TEARS

CHYNA had evolved into a completely new woman. Her union with Supreme was awkward. Part of her felt like she outgrew her twenty year long relationship with him. The big contradiction was the fact that he sponsored her evolution. He had paid her tuition at York College where she maintained a 4.0 average, and graduated at the top of her class. Now she was studying to take the Bar exam to become an attorney while working as a paralegal for the distinguished law firm of Herman & Schultz.

Chyna was looking for a way out of the 'hood, or rather the lifestyle that came with it. She yearned for an end to all of her sleepless nights where she worried about Supreme's whereabouts, and the pain she endured from his continuous adultery.

It was a constant dilemma because they lost their virginity together and grew up together. But they also had grown apart. She did not live in his world. She wanted to be legit. She hated all the violence, drugs and the hazardous lifestyle as Supreme became more deeply entrenched in the drug underworld.

Chyna sat in her home with tears flowing down her face. Her every fear was coming to fruition. There was an insatiable rumbling in her stomach. Butterflies were swirling around in her gut.

There was a loud knock at the door. She grabbed her nickel-plated automatic 38 caliber handgun and walked to the door with the gun pointed straight ahead of her. "Who the fuck is it?" she demanded.

"It's me, 'Preme! Open the fucking door!" Supreme yelled from the other side of the door.

Chyna opened the door. "Where the fuck were you, 'Preme? And why the fuck do you only have your boxers on?" she asked heatedly.

Supreme laughed and said, "Just give me $100 real quick."

Chyna was furious and yelled while she went to her Michael Kors pocketbook and pulled out a hundred dollar bill, "Oh my God! You're a fucking stupid motherfucker! You come to my house banging on my fucking door all crazy, and you ain't got no fucking clothes on! 'Preme, what the fuck!"

Supreme took the money and said, "I'll be right back." He went to pay the cab driver, jogged back inside and slammed the door closed.

Chyna was sitting on her plush leather couch with her arms folded. Streams of tears were flowing down her slender, golden-brown face. She narrowed her chinky eyes, which shrank even smaller to appear like little slits on her face. She squinted even harder, and with rage she looked into Supreme's eyes anticipating his lies. They had been here before all too often, and she was just about fed up with the nonsense. "I can't! I can't! I can't do this shit no more, 'Preme! You don't give a fuck about anybody but yourself! You're just a fucking selfish Black motherfucker!"

"What are you talking about, babe? Let me explain."

Chyna sat there rocking back and forth. Her lips quivered with every word. "Explain what? You mean sit here and believe another one of your lies?"

"What're you bitching 'bout? A little punk ass hundred dollars? I'll give you a G back. Fuck you want to beef over money after all I gave you!" Supreme shot back.

"Money? Money? Nigga, I don't give a fuck 'bout no money! I care about the constant lying, nigga! I called you thirty times! How was I supposed to know you're okay? You had me thinking you were dead! Then you come walking in here with blood on your shirt, barefoot and with only your boxers on! Come on, 'Preme! What happened?"

"Calm the fuck down and I'll tell you what happened!" He began stuttering. "I... I... I was at my boy's crib and niggas just rushed in—"

China interrupted him. "You fucking liar!" she yelled, and threw her gun at him, just missing his head. "Get the fuck out! You know you were at some bitch's house! You think I'm fucking stupid? Fuck you, nigga! Fuck you! Get the fuck out! I wish they would have killed you! Get out!"

Supreme became enraged. He rushed at Chyna and slammed her to the floor. "You stupid bitch! I told you what happened!"

"Yeah, I'm stupid, so I'm supposed to believe that you were at a nigga's house with your pants down? So what? You fucking niggas too?" she spat back at him.

The implication of homosexuality felt like a deeper insult. He cocked his fist back and grabbed Chyna's throat with his other hand.

"So you gonna choke me now 'Preme, huh? You gonna smash my face, huh? Is that what you did to her? Is that why niggas tried to kill you, huh 'Preme? I can't do this shit no more, 'Preme! I'm tired of the cheating, the lies, tired of not knowing if you're dead in the street!"

He let go of her neck and unballed his fist. "Babe, can you fucking relax? Can we talk? My day was too stressful for this shit!"

"Your day was stressful, nigga? I'm paranoid! It's like you're trying to kill me, putting your rusty little dick in all those bitches, and then coming home to me!"

"Oh boy! Here we go again with this shit! Listen—"

Chyna interrupted him, pointed a finger in his face and said. "No, you listen! I just lost my best friend behind you and dumb ass Freedom's bullshit!"

"Fuck is you saying?" Supreme asked.

Chyna's voice softened to a whisper. She looked perplexed as she stared into his face and asked, "So you don't know?"

"Know what?" he asked.

She got up and sat down on the couch and stared off into space as though she was daydreaming. "They killed Samaya! They chopped her body up, 'Preme!"

"Are you serious?"

Her eyes were bloodshot red as she trembled with a mixture of rage and anxiety. All she thought was how easily it could have been her. It could have been her mutilated body with her entrails scattered about. "Do I look serious? That could have been me, babe! I just got off the phone with her mother. She said it was so gruesome that they couldn't even piece the body together."

"Shit! Shit! Shit! What about Rain? Is she okay?" Supreme asked.

"She's with Samaya's mother. She's fine."

"Okay, okay. Damn, I got to think!" Supreme said, and began

pacing back in forth with his mind racing and contemplating on what to do next. Someone was playing very dirty.

Supreme found himself in a dark, cold place. His next move had to be an act of pure vehemence. There was no other alternative. Freedom would be devastated.

Supreme couldn't cry. His heart wouldn't allow it. Instead, he felt benumbed; his thoughts rigid and fierce. As he wrapped his arms around his lover to calm her shaking body, his soul grew heavy with the burden of warfare. A chill came over him. It was a feeling of pure bloodlust. Someone had to pay. All he could see was red, and the only name that came to his mind was *"Sopa!"*

CHAPTER 14

INCUBUS

FREEDOM *awoke in the middle of the night. Everyone else in his dorm lay asleep. He had heard a familiar female voice:*

"Jamaal!" she said in a whisper.

Freedom got up to follow her, but when he stood up, the floor was completely wet and sticky with blood.

"Jamaal!"

The familiar female in a ghostly white nightgown turned a corner, and Freedom began to pursue her. Every turn she made was fast and elusive. He wondered why no guards were present. At one point he started to call her name, but he couldn't speak and this puzzled him. But his mind shouted out, "Samaya! Samaya!"

He placed his hand under his nose only to realize with horror that he had no lips to move and no mouth to speak with.

Looking down, the sticky blood seemed to rise with every step he took as he wound his way through the prison, and he watched as his fellow prisoners drowned in their sleep. Why aren't they struggling? Why can't I scream!

Before he knew it, the crimson overflow had reached just above his neck, and he lost track of his mysterious siren. Now completely mortified by his visions, he thought to escape.

Off in the distance he noticed popping air bubbles in the blood, as if something was rising to the surface. Then, Samaya's blood-drenched head rose. Her eye sockets were completely removed and streams of fluid gushed forward. She screamed, "Jamaal!"

"Freedom! Freedom!" Mike said, pushing on Freedom's shoulder to awaken him.

Freedom woke up in shock. "What!?" He braced himself to strike Money Mike, but Mike quickly moved back and threw his hands up in a submissive posture.

"Easy, lil' bro! You was having a bad dream. You were shaking and calling someone named Somoya... Samaya?" Mike said.

Freedom stood up, body drenched in sweat. He looked around to get his bearings on reality. There was an uneasy feeling in his stomach, and something told him that it was not completely a dream.

Money Mike was a powerful individual in jail and outside of prison, so it was easy for him to keep a wireless Samsung cell phone. He would regularly let Freedom use it to make business calls to Supreme, his family, Samaya, etc.

"Let me use the phone, Mike."

"Why? Wassup, lil bro? You okay?" Mike asked.

"I got a funny feeling inside, man. I've got to call Samaya." Freedom's expression was frantic—almost desperate. He knew that something was wrong, and he had to be certain before jumping to any conclusions. He dialed Samaya's cell phone number. His mind was racing and his heart was pounding like he had a V-12 engine in his chest.

Samaya's phone rang four times in a row before he got an answer.

"Hello, Samaya?"

"No, Jamaal. Samaya is not here."

"Oh, okay, Umi. Is she okay?"

The name "Umi" means Mother in Arabic. Umi was Samaya's mother who was a street-wise older Muslim woman. She was very stern and strong willed. Freedom always showed Umi the utmost respect.

Generally Umi's tone was very flat and stoic. It never really fluctuated to express emotion, but now he could detect the obvious discontent in her when she asked, "Are you finally happy, Jamaal?"

"Happy about what?"

"Oh, so you don't know, huh?"

"Know what, Umi?"

"That Samaya's dead! They came to her home and murdered her and her husband!"

Freedom's legs grew weak. His heart dropped to his scrotum and his body felt numb. He couldn't believe what he was hearing.

"Yup, the police are still investigating. But we're sure it had something to do with her affiliation with you, you little black bastard! You succeeded in destroying my first child!"

Freedom started to speak. "Is... is... is Rain..."

"Yes, Rain is just fine, except for the fact that she will be traumatized for the rest of her life! The poor child came home from school and found her mother's body completely mutilated! You hear me, motherfucker! They chopped Samaya's body up because of you! That's supposed to be *your* body in the morgue, not hers! Oh, excuse me. Did I say body? Because actually there was hardly any of her left to identify her by her medical records! You don't deserve to have a Muslim name so honorable as Jamaal! There is nothing beautiful about you. You are a monster, and all of your associates are monsters! I can honestly say that I have never hated anyone, but you, Jamaal, I hope you die, Jamaal!"

Freedom was at a complete loss for words. There was ultimately nothing he could do, nor were there words he could say to show his empathy. Nor could he debate the truth of her murder being his fault. Someone wanted to send him a message of bloody carnage; a message that said, *"No one is safe! No one is safe at all!"* Whoever it was wanted to destroy him by picking him apart piece by piece, starting with his queen. This was a deadly game of chess, and Freedom was definitely in check.

"When you come out of jail, don't you come near Rain! To her you are just as dead as her mother is! I will not allow you to ruin my grandchild! I hope you are hurting like I am! I hope my despair and sorrow reverberates through this phone! I pray to Allah that it stifles, strangles and murders you in your sleep, you wretched little djinn! You have proven to be nothing more than a tool of Shaytan! Don't you ever call this phone or my phone again!"

"But, Umi…"

"What?!"

He only had one thing to say, because there was nothing else left in him. "I'm going to find the person that did this and—"

"I know what you're going to do, but that won't bring my child back!" Umi said, and hung up the phone.

Freedom calmly passed the cell phone back to Mike, who quickly stashed it away. He sat down on his bed and stared blankly at the wall as tears welled up in his eyes until they bubbled over and poured down his face. His love, sorrow and rage had all congealed into a state of equanimity. He completely zoned out, and like many adults in times of crisis, he had returned to his childlike state…

Jamaal was huddled up in the corner of Freedom's consciousness. He cowered in the corner of his mind and rolled his body into a ball. Hiding in the corner he cried, shivered and screamed at his older counterpart, "Why? Why? Why?"...

Freedom, the man kept his outer shell focused and sturdy as he searched for answers. He turned his focus inside, peering at his inner child cowering in the corner of his mind. But Freedom had no answers. He couldn't save the day. All he had was his sorrow and the flame of his anger. That flame scorched him inside until it consumed his entire being.

He turned to Mike with tears flooding his eyes, and in a very stoic tone he whispered, "They killed Samaya! I need to know who killed Samaya!"

CHAPTER 15

WOLF PACK

IT'S a strange wolf pack mentality how the Kitty Gang/PNA all related to each other while standing on the corner of 163rd and 89th Avenue, hustling their drugs and catcalling every young lady who walked by. This was the younger generation, and they had the body language of a group of hyenas. From a distance you would have thought of them as a disorganized bunch of hoodlums. On the contrary, they had a hierarchy with functioning job positions that rotated throughout the clique.

LA was what you would consider a general or a boss.

Gun Smoke was a ruthless killer/boss.

Gangsta Light (GL) was more of a bruiser and a block enforcer. He was the kind of individual who loved to fight any time, any day and anywhere. Originally he moved out to Queens from East New York where they were trying to kill him every day. The irony of it all was that GL wasn't in the least bit timid. He just wasn't the most likeable person in the world. He had moved to Queens with his mother and decided he would make his mark. Maybe it was the fact that he was half white, born from a white mother and a black father. He felt the need to prove himself a little extra.

LA recently just returned from a ten year bid, and took a liking to GL. GL was the only one who held down their block. GL really stood for "Gangsta Life", but everyone called him Gangsta *"Light"* behind his back.

LA, Gun Smoke and GL were the older guys who sort of linked up together, while Red, Elmo and Loopy Joe were the younger foot soldiers with their own set of ideals and ambitions. They actually had dreams of being a rap group called PNA.

Red was the more levelheaded one who orchestrated most of their shows and studio time. He came up with most of the concepts for their songs, while Loopy Joe was exactly what his name suggested: "loopy".

Young, fly and flashy with long braids that hung down to his shoulders, Loopy had his hands in a little bit of everything, from slinging E pills to pimping young girls on the strip down by Queens Boulevard.

All of these brothers were closely knit by one common fabric. They were all part of New York's Blood gang. There were different "sets" and "chapters" like the groups that LA and Gun Smoke belong to, which were "bounty hunters". This was a chapter of pure, coldblooded hitmen.

LA was a short, slim, dark-skinned assassin. He had earned his stripes banging in Compton, California. He came back to New York and quickly proved why he was a five-star general. He began recruiting for his own set, Kitty Gang, named after his code name for money, which is "kitty". Their slang was colorful and elaborate.

LA's right-hand was Gun Smoke. He was tall and skinny, but as deadly as his namesake. Gun Smoke was a bounty hunter… but then he wasn't. He was whatever he wanted to be, whenever he wanted to be. The pure cynicism of his existence was the fact that he was actually the son of a national chess champion. Gun Smoke had the I.Q. of a genius, but he camouflaged it in somewhat spontaneous behavior. His biggest secret was that he was actually very premeditated in all his actions.

Supreme never did quite understand or condone the entire gang culture that permeated throughout New York City, but he knew like anyone else on the street that you either roll with the tide, or get drowned by it, and no one man could change it. Even guys like Gun Smoke, who was an original 5-Percenter, found themselves being sucked up into the gang culture and lifestyle.

For brothers like LA, Gun Smoke and many others, it was a social status throughout New York and other states. It gave them the ability to move around freely in different neighborhoods without having to prove themselves everywhere they went. Being affiliated with a gang, having a reputation or a rank within a set created a sort of subculture, if you will. It was an underworld within the underworld where affiliates could quickly check your résumé and tell if you were about the life you were claiming.

Now of course you had those who were good at faking it, but faking it could only last so long because eventually you would be called to task. If at that point you proved to be less than what you claimed, then you became food for the pack.

On that particular day Supreme had called a meeting.

Everyone was outside. Usually there would have only been two or three of them at a time. They had a system that worked similar to a Fortune 500 company, and each hustler had his shift. There were three eight hour shifts, and on that corner you could get any drug you wanted.

It wasn't as if they rested when they weren't on the block either.

There were always tons of other duties that had to be fulfilled because they worked as wholesale distributers on behalf of Supreme and Kendu.

Supreme established his connection to the Kitty Gang through Lex, his long time ally.

Supreme rolled up on the block in an all black Denali jeep. Switching up vehicles was a habit of his. It was one of his ways of keeping the police and stickup kids off balance. He watched as the Kitty Gang and the PNA boys were up to their usual shenanigans.

GL was doing his usual enforcing on the block. "I don't give a fuck if y'all are waiting for Supreme! It's my shift, Scrap! Don't be trying to make sales on my shift!" he said with a menacing tone and standing at least two feet taller than Elmo, his short, slim adversary.

Elmo had just finished passing off a 3.5 gram bag of sour diesel weed to a customer. "Fuck outta here, nigga! I'm out-chere! That's my customer, nigga! He came to *me*!" he countered.

Elmo had his best friend, Joka with him. Joka was a Crip gang member, but that did not stop the two childhood buddies from being best friends. However, it would always cause conflict between their groups.

Elmo and Joka ate together, hustled together and put in work together despite GL's feelings.

"Elmo, I don't give a fuck if that was your custy (slang for customer)!" he said as he inched towards Elmo in a threatening manner.

Joka prepared himself to ambush GL from the side.

"And what the fuck's poppin' with the crab nigga out here all the time? I'm about to slap you *and* your little man!" GL shot back. ("Crab" is used by Bloods as a derogatory term for a Crip.)

LA rushed over to get in between GL and Elmo. "Calm down, Scrap! We got this meeting about to happen and we can't be dumbing out right now. We're going to hit the block up!" he said, and turned to Joka and gave him a look of affirmation. "You good, Scrap?" he asked him.

"I'm cool, Cuz. I'm about trappin' and rappin'. My G wants bread, not beef," Joka replied. He was witty with the slick talk and rhymes.

Supreme rolled down the window of his black Denali as he pulled up slowly. "Yo-o-o-o! What up? Why y'all niggas always fighting each other? Damn! Get in. Let's be out," he said.

LA, Elmo and Red jumped into the back seat, leaving GL, Loopy and Joka to work the block.

The meeting was what you might have considered a "mobile meeting". Supreme drove around the back streets of Jamaica, Queens with Kendu in the passenger seat and the others in the back, while he briefed them on exactly what was going on with them as a crew.

Basically, they were under attack. They knew nothing of what had happened to Samaya or the fact that Mercedes tried to set him up. He kept that between him, Kendu and Pistola. The word was that the Kitty Gang needed to be armed. The war was on. The Dominicans in La Compania were definitely coming—at least that was what Supreme surmised. Sangre de Jesus was outside of his purview.

The only good part of his briefing was the information that his right-hand man, Freedom would be coming home from prison very soon. Supreme didn't want Freedom to come home from jail and jump right back into the streets. He functioned perfectly fine without him.

Freedom was more like a beacon of hope; a white light at the end of the dark catacombs of street life. He had grown weary of the never-ending treadmill of dealing drugs and dishing out death. In Supreme's mind, Freedom had the answer. He could save them and legitimize them. But, the only catch was that Supreme didn't necessarily want to leave the street life alone. He wanted the glamor and glitz minus the hazards.

Supreme's plan was to start a record label with himself as the face of the business, and knowing that his partner would be all too comfortable in the background. Everything had to be airtight. No flaws allowed. Rules and regulations had to be strictly enforced, and transgressions would be met with swift and brutal penalties.

******

After a very informative meeting, Supreme dropped Elmo, LA and Red off, and he and Kendu drove to an after-hours spot to sniff a couple of lines of cocaine and discuss business.

The after-hours parties were always in an undisclosed location. That particular night it was held at The Tropical Inn, on Francis Lewis Boulevard. The parties always started about 3:00 a.m. Partygoers always consisted of A-list hustlers in Jamaica Queens.

Mook Diamond was one of the biggest promoters in New York City, and his after-hour events were his way of giving back to his hood. He always had some of the nastiest, no holds barred exotic dancers present, mixed in with some of South Jamaica Queens' most notorious drug dealers.

"...I smell a pussy from a block away,
Let's shoot them pussies from a block away.
They wanna see a nigga in a cage,
Baby mama garnishing a nigga's wage.
I just went and got the Chevy sprayed,
Pussy nigga want a scratch a nigga's paint.
Pussy nigga want to see you fall,
Just know to bring the choppers when you see me call..."

Rick Ross' song rattled the speakers while DJ Superstar Jay worked his laptop, and every stripper made their butt cheeks quake to the feverish tempo of the music. The strobe lights danced off of each patron's jewelry.

The music paused for a brief moment, and DJ Superstar Jay said, "Okay, okay, okay, ladies! Time to turn it up! Big Kendu, Supreme and the C.M.K. Money Gang boys are in the building! Big shout out!"

Supreme responded with a head nod and walked directly through the crowd straight to the bar. Kendu walked slowly behind him, bumping his way through the crowd and exchanging handshakes and hugs. They felt the love, but the hate was thicker than the rich clouds of marijuana smoke. There was a unique aroma. It was a mixture of vaginal secretions and weed in the air.

Killers were lurking in the shadows, but none wanted to violate Mook Diamond. He had that love. Everyone kept the peace, at least while inside the club.

Chocolate Chyna Doll from Kay Slay's *Straight Stuntin'* magazine was bartending, and she knew Supreme well. She automatically passed him two bottles of Hennessey Privilege, and he in turn pulled out a wad of cash, peeled off three one-hundred dollar bills and slapped them on the bar top. He then winked at Chyna Doll and walked away.

Kendu already had a table. He was sitting with Lex. There was a certain amount of comfort knowing that Lex was there, because wherever he went, so did multiple guns.

Supreme sat down, passed Kendu a bottle and asked with a smirk on his face, "Nigga, why you always wearing shades at night?"

Kendu just grinned behind his Cartier shades and said, "These ain't shades, nigga. These are hater blockers for niggas like you!"

"Fuck outta here, you old Al B. Sure ass nigga!"

Lex didn't even grin.

"Yo, Lex, wassup?" Kendu asked.

"Nothing, nigga. I'm about to jam one of these niggas up."

"Nah, don't do that at Mook's shit," Supreme told him.

"Fuck Mook! He's lucky it ain't him!" Lex shot back.

Kendu invited Supreme to follow him into the bathroom. He pulled out a hundred-dollar bill with some coke in it.

Supreme had changed since he got with Kendu and Lex. He had developed a cocaine habit. He was what you would call a "weekend warrior", disciplining himself to only sniff on Friday and Saturday nights. His excuse to himself was that he needed it to stay on point. It kept him alert and aggressive.

Kendu and Lex had turned him onto coke, but the stress of the streets had turned him out. Snorting cocaine started off as something Supreme did on the weekends for social use. But soon it became an everyday habit, along with a cocktail of other drugs like Ecstasy pills, OxyContin's, Percocet's and Vicodin's.

Supreme was an escapist and was doing anything he could to escape reality. The ultimate reality was that he had gotten in way too deep, and the walls were closing in on him. His relationship with Chyna was a complete duality of love mixed with hate. As much as he cared for her, in his heart he felt conflicted. He could never get over the betrayal of her dealings with Cash.

He also felt uneasy around his new set of friends. Their comradery didn't come from a genuine place. With the Money Gang and the Kitty Gang, it was about the money first, then came the loyalty, trust and friendship. He felt like a lion leading a pack of young hyenas, and at any given time they could turn around and decide that he was their prey.

The good old days with Freedom and Fire was rooted in true friendship. Back then, the need to be financially stable took them into crime, but their foundation was brotherhood. Even with a foundation solidified by a brotherly bond, they still ended up divided. So, what were the hopes for this newly formed union?

Supreme had one thing he could trust, and that was his ability to hustle. And Freedom was a true comrade. Even so, the cliché that absence makes the heart grow fonder has its flaws in regards to friendship. He often contemplated that Freedom would come out of jail a different man. Judging by his letters, it seemed like Freedom went through some type of spiritual awakening. All of his letters described this new metaphysical utopia that he had found. Freedom had acclimated himself to the literary works of John Henry Clarke and Dr. Yosef Ben-Jochannan. In a nutshell, he was in jail changing, and Supreme was very uneasy about it.

Freedom's letters also hinted of getting out of the game. Supreme loved the fast money, cars and designer clothes, along with the notoriety and the stares and whispers of all who were around when he walked into a club, a room or down the street. Supreme loved being Supreme, and his dream was to achieve "supremacy". All Freedom wanted to do was be "free".

Kendu and Supreme were in the men's bathroom, sniffing up a storm.

"Yo, 'Preme! Yo, 'Preme! Stop daydreaming, nigga. I got to tell you some shit," Kendu said.

"Huh? What up, God? This is some good ass 'Tony'!" (Slang for cocaine, derived from the fictional character, Tony Montana from the movie "Scarface".)

"That's exactly what the fuck I want to talk about. I got a call from Don-Don earlier."

"Oh, okay. So what the fuck is that Haitian nigga talking about now?" Supreme asked.

Kendu let out a deep breath in frustration before he spoke. "Man, he's talking 'bout he got some type of drought shit going on. He said he's not gonna be able to hit us with the same price no more."

"Fuck! How much is he talking?"

"Twenty-five wholesale."

"That's crazy! Get the fuck outta here! Wassup with that nigga?"

Kendu shook his head and said, "I don't even know, my nigga."

"Nah, God, this don't seem right. I don't trust that mother-fucker. He raised the price by four stacks a kilo. We gotta fix that nigga. I just got to figure this shit out."

"So, what're we gonna do?" Kendu asked.

"We gotta find a new connect. Wassup wit' B. Black from the barbershop?"

"I'ma have to check wit' that nigga," Kendu replied.

"Alright, cool. I'ma check wit' Pistola and see if he got any connects uptown."

As the two comrades walked out of the bathroom, the strobe and laser light effects seemed to create a hypnotic sense of doom. Supreme could feel the death in the air. He had an eerie feeling come over him.

"Why would Don-Don turn on them after he had spent hundreds of thousands with him? Why did Mercedes set me up? Was she alive or dead?" Supreme wondered.

As they sat down, Lex followed a drug dealer into the bathroom with his eyes. He seemed to be scanning for victims.

Lex's long silky braids seemed to form a cloak over his slender dark facial features. He resembled a Black Jesus with sinister eyes.

Supreme had a very intimate friendship with Lex; a dark history of multiple capers. Their inaudible connection allowed them to read one another's thoughts. Supreme could see the predator in Lex's eyes, like a salivating tiger stalking its prey.

"Lex, I know you ain't about to get a nigga here in the spot," Supreme said to him.

Lex said in a calm, monotone voice even as he yelled above the music, "Yes, I am about to get one of these niggas. That nigga right there's looking like food."

"Lex, we got too much shit going on wit' us to be adding more drama."

"Look, Scrap. You're right. Too much shit's going on. So before niggas even start thinking it's sweet, I'ma start getting at niggas. Faggots respect pressure. I'm putting pressure on these niggas. They need to know that we ain't playing."

Patrons had just finished making it rain on a group of strippers, and before Supreme could respond, Lex stood up and followed the poor unsuspecting party.

The man had to have at least five thousand dollars or more on him. He was like a poor unsuspecting baby bison who had wandered away from the herd. Stumbling drunk and unaware of the danger that lurked in the mire, he staggered into the bathroom with his pockets overflowing with cash, and a long diamond chain dangling from his neck. He stood over the urinal relieving himself until the shock ensued.

Lex had followed him into the bathroom, and his attack was swift, accurate and unrelenting. He kicked the poor guy in the back with his size twelve Polo boots and pistol whipped him in the back of his neck until he lost consciousness. His face was split open and gushing blood all over the white porcelain. Had the music not been so loud, everyone might have heard the ruckus.

Lex quickly took all the cash out of the man's pocket and pulled the diamond studded 36" chain off his victim's neck. He rushed out of the bathroom, only to find Supreme standing in front of the door playing lookout.

Then Kendu, Supreme and Lex pushed and shoved their way through the crowd and rushed out the door.

CHAPTER 16

SABALI

"...Some of the smartest dummies,
Can't read the language of Egyptian mummies.
And a flag on the moon,
But can't find food for the starving tummies..."

THE song, "Patience" by Nas and Damian Marley played in the background as Money Mike and Freedom played one last game of chess before his release.

After thirteen long intense years, Freedom is finally being released. During his time in the federal penitentiary system, he had seen and learned many things.

Mike had become a mentor of some sort. He gave Freedom guidance and protection. They had formed a bond that could only be shared by a father and son. Freedom ever so fondly called him "Uncle Mike".

Mike had a lot of connections on the outside. These were all connections that his young protégé would need. He would be starting from scratch. He had no more money left in the streets except for the money that he was being released with.

His mind bore the burden of evolution. He had contemplated

just getting a legal job, but that wasn't him. He needed some sort of jumpstart. He knew that he wasn't ready to jump right back into the "street life". Hustling and selling drugs was a means to an end for him. It was not the opposite, as in an end to his means. How was he to get out of the lifestyle unscathed?

"Checkmate, young Jedi!" Mike said with a pseudo Yoda impersonation. Adding insult to injury, he added, "The force is great with this one. But unfortunately, you are not ready! So, what's up, King? You're about to be up out of here, so stop stressing. I told you I got you."

"It's just that I know how Supreme is. He's gonna want me to jump back in that shit. I'ma just need some time to myself to meditate and become acclimated to society."

"Exactly! You're right on track. Now listen. I have a niece named Nefertarie. She knows all about you. She's going to look out for you; help you get a job. She'll teach you more of the metaphysical sciences. You have a long journey ahead of you, Freedom." Mike's eyes were big, fiery coals that could melt a person. Those piercing eyes in the middle of his bulb-like head only further complimented his regal Olmec features.

"Mike, I don't want to be a burden on you and your family."

"It's not about you; it's about us organizing this movement. You have greater things to do with your life. You are a living example of alchemy, transforming iron into gold. Just focus on getting things together. Plus, I need you to do me a couple of favors."

Freedom had evolved into a whole new individual. His spiritual awareness had grown exponentially. He spent his time either reading, exercising, or planning. Mike would stay up late with him, mentoring him. They would have an infinitude of crucial debates about everything from religion to politics.

Mike never had a son, so Freedom had become the closest thing to a son for him. He wanted to help Freedom by giving him the gift of self-knowledge. It was a gift that can overpower anything. It would not prevent a man from getting locked up, but it could prevent a man for staying locked in.

Freedom had discovered a hidden part of himself. He became a scholar and connoisseur of fine literature that spoke on the African diaspora. He saw how much racial discrimination affected his everyday life. He found great purpose in the idea of changing his life for the better. He wanted to be so effective that he could change the lives of those closest to him.

Even in his brief moments of serenity, Freedom was terrorized by images of war. He was mentally prepared to leave the streets completely, but with Samaya's murder, he could not let go. He had to avenge her. He had to make a point that infractions could not go unpunished. So, as much as he wanted out, he had to stay in.

He had become obsessed with his spirituality. His thirst for knowledge had gone unquenched for years. The 5-Percent lessons gave him pride and focus. Islam was his foundation; like a springboard to assist him in diving into every aspect of occult wisdom.

Some months before Freedom was released, he began experimenting with his dreams and the reopening of his pineal gland through meditation.

Mike was a high ranking Voodoo priest as well as an active Master Mason. His intentions were to make Freedom his initiate, but Freedom was reluctant to commit to any fraternal organization.

Rumors of the "dark sciences" being linked to the Illuminati and other types of conspiracies made him precarious about their studies.

There were three deciding factors that had pushed Freedom in the direction of studying the occult.

Some years back, early into his bid, he had a heated argument with Mike about spirituality and religion. Mike began to teach him to go beyond his lessons and yet familiarize himself with African deities and ancestral connections.

Freedom had taken everything as blasphemous devil worship until Mike told him one thing. He had said, "Did you ever watch an autopsy? No? Well, the thing about an autopsy is that they search the entire body for the cause of death. Once they have gone through every means of research and they don't find a cause of death, what is the last place they check?"

Freedom just shrugged his shoulders in naïveté.

"They check the fecal matter. They dig through the shit. You have dug into spirituality. You have dug in the light. But remember; light can only come out of darkness."

"So, what are you telling me? You on some Voodoo shit?" Freedom asked him.

"No, I'm on some Black shit; some original man shit; some God shit. Y'all niggas say y'all are gods, but when it comes to doing god shit, y'all turn into bitches," Mike said, and laughed with a sinister chuckle. He then went on to explain, "You, my son, are placing a Christian motif on ancient sciences that existed thousands of years before the inception of Christianity."

"Yeah, but I never said I was a Christian, or that I believed in all that Jesus stuff."

Mike chuckled like a proud parent observing his child's first steps.

"You may not be a Christian, but society has a way of structuring things so that the masses perceive things from a Christian oriented paradigm. For instance, the bad guy wears black, and the good guys wear white. Angels are always depicted in all white. The word 'media' comes from the Greek god Medea, which was the god of illusion. So even though we might reject certain images or concepts consciously, we still tend to absorb them subconsciously. Your subconscious is your higher self and controls all of your higher functions. It is your 'dark side', and from dark comes light."

Freedom nodded his head in understanding.

"Freedom, do you fear men?"

"No!"

Mike peered deeply into his eyes. "So why then would you fear the spirit? Why would you fear the dark? Why would you fear yourself?" he asked.

It was that conversation that changed Freedom's mindset altogether, and sparked his enthusiasm for "black magic". The more he focused, the more intense his dreams had become. He would often see skulls in his nightmares. The vision of a skull-faced man wearing a purple suit would pollute his restless nights. Freedom took this as a challenge, and in his sleep he managed to muster up the strength to confront the skull-faced gentleman:

"Who are you?" he would ask.

In a haunting baritone hiss, the skull-faced man responded, *"I am you!"*

Ever since that night, Freedom never saw that vision again, and he never spoke of it to Mike.

Knowledge is a blessing, but it is also a responsibility. There is a saying that "God protects babies and fools." Freedom was neither. He kept his release date quiet. No one knew when he was coming home from jail, but from jail to the streets, his name was so big that a lot of people had an idea, but no exact date.

When Officer Mullins came to get him to discharge him, Freedom turned to Mike and hugged him as both fought back tears.

Freedom walked down the aisle of his dorm staring blanking and giving head nods to all the Bloods, Crips, G.D.'s, Vice Lords, 5-Percenters, Muslims, and MS-13 members. What hurt was the fact that no matter how diverse the gangs were, culturally they were all the same. There were black and brown men that made up over half the prison population.

As fast as he tried to walk, his feet felt heavy. His mind was weighed down with a basket of burdens. At the very bottom of the basket was Rain, his pride and joy whom hadn't come to visit him in five years. He knew that she loved him, but she also resented him for his poor choices in life that ultimately took both of her parents away. He wanted to be a real father to her, but first he had to be a real man for himself.

There was also the dilemma of finding out who killed Samaya. He was a towering inferno of rage inside, and the guilt of her death alone would have brought him to the point of suicide if he did not have Rain to live for.

The other burden was the streets. He had made a vow that he was C.M.K., but his mind was in a different place. He wanted to take his business acumen and apply it to a legal hustle.

As he walked down the corridor in his gray sweat suit and fresh gray New Balance Classics, his stomach churned in anticipation after thirteen years of confinement. There was a slight fear of the outside world. He had spent his young adult years incarcerated. Anxiety would grip the most level-headed person. It had been thirteen years since he had been with a woman; thirteen years since he'd been able to defecate in privacy; and thirteen years since he'd interacted with anyone other than officers and criminals. He had prayed, meditated and focused. He vowed to himself that he would not be another statistic.

******

It was about a three hour ride to New York, and the difference between his hometown and the scenic suburban look of Philly was astronomical.

Freedom walked around midtown Manhattan looking at the skyscrapers. It was an overdose of stimuli of the honking horns of buses and cars, and the rumbling of the trains underground vibrating the concrete under his feet. Hustlers walked about whispering, "Sour bud!" "Loosies!"

Everything was different to him. The streets had changed. It seemed like everyone had futuristic cell phones and wore tight clothes; even the men. The music was different. He wondered if the culture evolved, or did it dissolve.

Things that would repulse the average New Yorker felt like heaven to Freedom. He rejoiced in the scent of car exhaust mixed with pretzels, hotdogs and caramelized peanuts.

Despite being over a decade without a cigarette, Freedom relapsed. It was the nostalgia of being home. A sip of rum or even a couple of pulls of some weed would have ultimately been better, but he had a limited amount of time to report to the halfway house in Brooklyn. As an obligation of his federal sentence, he would have to stay there for six months. He took his time enjoying his cigarette, and was momentarily dazed by the head rush. That first cigarette in thirteen years had left him with a wicked head rush that reminded him of why he had quit in the first place.

Finally, he arrived at 988 Myrtle Avenue to check himself into the Brooklyn CCC, up the block from Tompkins Projects.

The halfway house was clean and sanitary. There were four men to each room, one or two bathrooms on each floor, but it still wasn't freedom. It was a taste of freedom, but it was still just a jail to him. There was a 10:00 p.m. curfew, he was subject to random urine tests, and he had to get a job or be obligated to attend all types of programs.

Freedom enjoyed a moment of solitude as he lay on his bunkbed staring at the ceiling and pondering his next move. As much as he had an abundance of aspirations, nothing could take place until he fixed his current situation. The last thing he wanted was to contact Supreme. He needed to be a ghost until he figured things out.

He was definitely going to contact his mother, but he wanted a couple of days to settle in. He needed to contact someone.

As much as Freedom wanted to be independent, he knew that he needed help. But he wanted it to be someone neutral. That's when he shuffled through his folder containing the pencil drawn designs for his Necessary Evil T-shirt brand. He sifted through notes about Kabballah and his personal memoirs for a book he was playing with writing and found Nefertarie's address and phone number. Calling her was his only option. He had to start fixing his life.

CHAPTER 17

THE EASTERN STAR

"...You are my African Queen,
The girl of my dreams.
You take me where I never been,
You make my heart go ting-a-ling-a-ling.
Yeah..."

"AFRICAN Queen" by 2Face Idibia was playing over the sound system of Nu Tribe Hair Salon located on Gold Street in downtown Brooklyn, right off of Fulton Street. The decor and vibration in the salon was very serene and peaceful. It was filled with spiritual statues from many indigenous cultures. A small clay mound with cowry shells for eyes and a mouth sat in a bowl near the front entrance. Candies and coins were placed inside the bowl. The walls were adorned with wooden African masks.

Nu Tribe Salon specialized in natural hairstyles. They did everything from locks to braids, and haircuts.

The shop owner and manager was Nefertarie, Money-Mike's niece.

Nefertarie stood about five feet seven inches, and was 170 pounds of voluptuous Amazonian flesh. The sides of her head were shaved in a Mohawk style, and she had long, silky, jet-black dread-locks that draped down to her curvaceous buttocks. Her eyes were large, dreamy and deep-set with an Asian slant. Her features were primitive yet majestic, with full pink lips. Her beauty was rich and exotic yet foreign. Her ethnic background was a mixture of a Haitian mother and Trinidadian father.

She was wearing a loose fitting purple dashiki, tight fitting True Religion jean shorts, and purple and pink Nike Airforce 1's.

While waiting for Freedom's arrival, Nefertarie was doing her usual interlocking a customer's hair, treating it with Moringa Oil and Black Seed. She was a gifted hairstylist, loctician, and a master at dealing with Black hair. She was a trichologist of some sort, beauti-fying and strengthening her people's hair with well-honed skills and techniques that she had developed over the years.

But Nefertarie had more to her than just being a beautician. She was a witch; a high priestess well versed in the "black arts". Born in Haiti, she had gotten her introduction into Voodoo by her uncle and mother.

As she grew wiser and gained knowledge, she became a theoso-phist, traveling the world in the name of "Black Liberation". Her journeys had taken her to places like Togo and Benin where she studied some of the origins of Ifá, an ancient African system of divination that is at the core of many spiritual systems like Yoruba, Santeria, Voodoo and Vodun, and Palo Mayombe.

Her travels were furnished by her uncle's drug money, and in exchange for his financial assistance, she managed a chain of hair salons that laundered his money.

Nefertarie was Mike's best kept secret, and no matter how many associates he had trusted, no one knew who she was. That was how she knew Freedom was someone her uncle held in high esteem. So, when she finally received a phone call from her uncle's protégé whom she had heard so much about, she welcomed him with open arms.

Freedom didn't know what to expect regarding Nefertarie. Psychologically he was in a very secluded and lonely place. He just needed someone to confide in and who could assist him with re-entering into society.

After he walked into Nu Tribe Salon, every woman inside stopped to observe his six foot tall, dark reddish-brown chiseled frame. "Hello, ladies. I'm looking for Nefertarie," he announced.

"Yes, hello, King," she said.

For the first time in his life, Freedom felt like a sex object as the women gawked at him while he walked to the back of the salon.

Freedom stretched out his hand to shake Nefertarie's, but instead she leaned in and gave him a warm embrace. "So, how long have you been home?" she asked.

"I got out yesterday."

"Where're you staying?"

"I'm at a halfway house on Myrtle. I'm gonna have to stay there for like six months."

"You're going to need a job to get them crackers off your back."

"Yep."

"Okay, let's go in the back and talk."

The beauty salon had a little back yard with benches and a grill.

Nefertarie's stride was so divine that her hips swayed like she was a Black Venus in the flesh. Freedom was extremely attracted to her, but he maintained his composure out of respect for Mike.

As they settled in the backyard, Nefertarie explained to Freedom the work that needed to be done around the shop. She decided to give him a job opening and closing the salon and handling the maintenance. They both knew that this job wouldn't be anything permanent, but simply a front to get him through the next six months. They agreed that Freedom would open the shop, mop, sweep and take out the trash.

In the middle of their conversation she mumbled something under her breath.

"Excuse me, Sis, but what did you just say?" Freedom asked her.

"Nothing, Brother," she said, subtly trying to brush it off.

"Listen. I could have sworn I heard you say something."

Nefertarie sighed because she did not want to scare him, but there was something about him that she had to reveal. "I said, 'Is *he* always with you?'"

"Is who always with me?"

"So, you don't see him? You don't sense a presence or energy lingering around you?"

"Sometimes it's like I see shit out of the corner of my eye, but what or who exactly are you talking about?"

Nefertarie was born with a gift. She was a seer. She would have visions, dreams, even nightmares of things to come. Things that were invisible to most folks' eyes had a tendency of revealing themselves to her. The crazy thing about a higher sense of awareness was that it was both a gift and a curse. She saw things that she couldn't share because many of her visions were too intense to express, and often she could not shut the noise out of her head. She was a conduit and liaison to the spirit world.

"He is the Baron-Bawon Samedi, to be exact," she responded.

Freedom was studying hard, and he was very knowledgeable

when it came to ancient Egyptian deities and historical figures, but that's sort of where his knowledge stopped. Despite evolving into a spiritual erudite, he still wasn't ready for certain levels of the occult.

Freedom felt a chill, and his arm hair stood up, but not from apprehension. There was something mysteriously enticing about Nefertarie's eyes and the way her Trinidadian accent rolled off her tongue. There was something that was pushing him forward, seducing his curiosity. In a calm monotone he asked, "Who is this Baron? What do you mean by he's always with me?"

"Have a seat, baby," Nefertarie said and gently grasped his hand and had him sit down on the bench. "Baron Samedi is Baron Saturday. He is a spirit from the Vodun Pantheon. He rules over death, healing and resurrection."

Freedom's curiosity had been sparked, but he still did not quite believe her. So, he tried to dig deeper into her psyche. He leaned in closer to her and asked, "So, why would this spirit stick so close to me?"

"Well truthfully speaking, my love, you have an army of spirits and ancient ancestors who watch over you. It's just at this particular phase of your life, he is with you."

"So, death is near?"

Nefertarie giggled and looked at Freedom as if he was a naïve child. "No, sweetie. I don't know why everyone gets caught up in the whole death thing. Just for you to die, he has to accept you. But more so than death, he presides over endings and beginnings. You are probably entering a new phase of your life. You have found new purpose. For this new purpose, these spirits and ancestors have sort of covered you with protection. Now, it is your job to stay in tune with these forces."

"Wow! That's some deep shit. I don't know if I'm ready for all that," Freedom said.

"Nefertarie gently placed her hands on top of his and told him, "If you weren't ready, you would not be here."

In that solitary moment, Freedom realized that he would never be the same. Another person would have heard her words and thought that she was some spooked out weirdo. Somehow, every word she said seemed to speak to his heart.

The word "information" is basically a compound word. The prefix "in" and the word "formation" gives the idea that information is actually formed on the inside. So no matter what advanced science you may have read or heard, it will not penetrate your psyche unless there is something inside you that was predisposed to vibrate on that frequency.

Freedom was onto Nefertarie's vibration, and as he stared into her eyes, warmth came over him and he found her utterly attractive. He thought to bask in the wealth of information his secret pseudo-sexual attraction was bestowing upon him. One of the greatest jewels she gave him was that it was time for him to learn forgiveness and uplifting himself.

They spoke until it was almost his curfew time, and Freedom went back to the halfway house. He stayed up all night trying to figure out Nefertarie and her words. Staring up at the ceiling, he kept rewinding his conversation with her, and the words kept repeating in his head:

"Forgiveness and uplifting himself. Focus on uplifting people and helping them rise. Forgiveness doesn't necessarily change your course of actions, but it can help you heal when you forgive."

Her advice was open-ended. She did not offer much of an explanation. Her profound words were more like clues.

CHAPTER 18

FORGIVENESS

H E had aged well, being in his mid-50's but resembling a man in his late 30's.

Gentrification was the latest epidemic to hit Harlem. Musa's hometown was a haven for Black revolutionaries and the Black social elite.

Harlem had a rich history of being a beacon for African American stars and business owners alike. What other place on Earth can say that it has housed the likes of Malcolm X, Dr. Maya Angelou and Puff Daddy? Despite the dilapidated buildings, this mecca of Black consciousness had been a Black ghetto heaven for decades, only to be bought out by folks who weren't tied to the community's heritage due to covert racism through economic discrimination.

Musa was the last man standing in his building at 515 West 148th Street. He was taking his Jewish landlord to court. Musa hadn't been paying rent for two years straight and had been wrestling with the landlord who was trying to evict the tenants and raise the rent. But since Musa was the one tenant who had lived there for over twenty years, he had a right to protest the rent increase.

Musa's apartment was filled with papers and pro-Black literature. He was recovering from hip surgery, but managed to get himself to a point where he could do calisthenics. He was a muscular man who was very fit for his age. He stood 5"10' tall, and had a full salt and pepper beard.

******

1981:

Musa and his brother, Mustafa were sitting at the table in Margie's apartment in Brooklyn.

Margie was wearing black tights, Pro-Keds and thick ankle socks, and a gray off-the-shoulder sweatshirt. Her long, thick curly hair was pulled into a high ponytail. She was in relax mode.

Musa was wearing a black Members Only jacket and fitted Guess jeans.

Mustafa was the flashy one. He was wearing a red velour Fila suit, red Fila sneakers, and a big rope chain that hung down to his bellybutton. When he smiled, he displayed a plethora of 14-karat gold fronts that adorned his teeth. Every one of his fingers was adorned with gold.

You could tell that Mustafa and Musa were polar opposites. While Musa went to college on a track scholarship, worked two jobs on the side and struggled to make ends meet, Mustafa was a well-known drug dealer who moonlighted as a bodyguard for some of the popular hip-hop artists of that day. But despite their differences and ever-present sibling rivalry, the brothers still had a level of reverence and respect for one another.

Mustafa admired his brother's intelligence and ambitions, and Musa admired his brother's courage and willingness to protect his family.

On this particular day, the three of them were just hanging out, watching television.

"I swear, one day Musa's going to be like George Jefferson!" Mustafa said jokingly.

Musa nudged Margie and said, "Oh no. I'ma be much more successful than him, right Margie?"

She nodded in reassurance.

Mustafa looked down at his rings. "I already moved up to a deluxe apartment in the sky!" he sang, mocking the theme song from the show "The Jefferson's".

"So why are you still staying at Mommy's house?" Musa asked.

"'Cause she be needing help, that's why."

The trio simultaneously broke out in laughter.

"Plus, I be getting money out here in these streets," Mustafa added. He pulled out a gram of coke wrapped up in a dollar bill. "I bet y'all ain't never seen nobody fuck with this," he said. Then he took a hundred dollar bill that he had rolled up tight and snorted a couple of lines in front of them.

Margie's eyes lit up with curiosity. Frankly, the fact that such a regal-like, tall, powerful brother draped in jewelry was sniffing made it look appealing. There was a glamour and mystique associated with cocaine, much like cigarettes.

There was no face that represented the tragedy of drug abuse. Just like the idea of a crack head and the visual parallel was yet to exist; just like there were no cigarette smokers with lung cancer to constitute how ugly the tobacco industry really was.

Musa wasn't impressed in the least bit.

"So, y'all wanna try it," Mustafa asked them.

"No, we're okay," Musa responded while giving Margie a stern look.

"She looks like she wants to give it a try, just once."

Musa turned to Margie and asked, "You really want to try that stupid shit, don't you?"

Margie nodded yes like a child.

"Okay, go ahead," Musa said in a very apprehensive tone.

That moment had proven to be one of the biggest mistakes of their lives. From that day forward, Margie steadily became more and more addicted to the illegal white substance.

Mustafa secretly fed it to her, and it was not out of larceny either. It was his way of having his family. He eventually got her into the business. He used her apartment as a stash house and made her a runner and delivery person for him. Rather than pay her in cash, he paid her in drugs.

Musa was back and forth to college, so it took him a while to really figure out what was going on. He began to notice Margie getting slimmer and her circle of friends had changed. And when his son, Jamaal seemed to look unattended and sores from his eczema were getting out of hand, that's when he intervened.

Musa was rifling through her pocketbook, looking for drugs.

"What the fuck are you doing, Musa? Get the fuck out of my shit! Ain't no nigga's number in there!" Margie shouted.

"That's not what I'm looking for!"

Jamaal stood close by. His eyes filled with tears. He didn't quite understand what was going on, but in his eyes his Dad was the "bad guy".

Musa pulled a small manila envelope of coke out of Margie's

pocketbook. "This is what the fuck I was looking for!" He then proceeded to flush it down the toilet.

Margie followed him into the bathroom, yelling and cursing. She couldn't even see what she had become. The drugs were stealing her youth.

Enraged, Musa shouted, "Who the fuck is giving you this shit?"

Margie's hesitation was answer enough. He draped her up but resisted the urge to slap her. As he quickly stomped out of the apartment he shouted, "I'll be back for my son!"

He headed directly for his mother's house. His mother, Rosetta, lived two train stops away on Church Avenue, in Brooklyn. She was a strong willed older Black woman who struggled to raise eight children as a single parent.

Musa was the oldest, and he was the father figure to his siblings. Musa and Mustafa financially supported their household. But the two brothers were nothing alike, and would often butt heads battling for alpha male supremacy.

Musa had gone away to Delaware State College, visiting on weekends and holidays, while Mustafa was in and out of prison. They were like Cain and Abel. Their mutual resentments were rooted in their conflicting lifestyles.

Musa lived his life on the straight and narrow. He followed the tenets of great pro-Black leaders like Marcus Garvey, Malcolm X and Martin Luther King, Jr. Despite institutionalized racism and the lack of opportunities for young Black males, Musa still believed that with hard work, and a good education, you can go far in life.

Mustafa's mentality was different from his brother's. He was a gangster who dropped out of high school in the 9th grade. Money, sex, clothes and drugs were his top priority.

Mustafa a.k.a. Big Muse was a terror at an early age, and his 52-Hand Block fight style struck fear in the hearts of his peers. As much as he was considered an official Black gangster on the streets of New York, in Rosetta's home he wasn't Big Muse. He was just Mustafa.

Musa's big/little brother was into all types of criminal activities, but kept it away from his mother's house, which was a get-away for him. On any given day they might wake up to find Muse curled up on Rosetta's living room couch in a fetal position and sucking his thumb.

On that particular day, Musa came barging into the apartment with a look of pure rage in his eyes. He was furious. He specifically told his brother not to give Margie any more drugs, only to find out that his brother went behind his back.

When he saw Mustafa lying on the couch, his first thought was to strike him in his sleep, but he still wanted to give him a fighting chance. His little brother was a lot bigger than he was, and while Musa was pretty much physically fit from being a track star, Mustafa was more muscular from long stints in prison where he became somewhat of a bodybuilder, and was impeccable in hand-to-hand combat.

In the middle of the living room sat a large television with a hanger connected to the back as an antenna. You had to smack the side of the set when the reception was bad.

Mustafa was lying there snoring loudly like a hibernating bear. Over ten thousand dollars' worth of jewelry lay on the coffee table next to the slumbering giant.

The flame of Musa's rage cut through the sweet scent of home-made cornbread. He quietly leaned over his brother and slapped him right in the face, knocking the thumb out of his mouth and completely stunning him.

Mustafa jumped up instantly. "What the fuck is wrong with you?" he asked while holding the side of his face.

"Motherfucker, I told you to stop giving Margie that poison!"

Mustafa knew that his brother was right, but his pride was hurt and he had to respond. He delivered two devastating blows to his brother's body that folded his slim frame and sent him careening into the love seat.

Musa instinctively stood right up, knowing that his brother was clearly stronger than he was. He grabbed one of his old track trophies off of the coffee table and lunged at his brother with the speed and agility of a cheetah. He swung the trophy wildly, and barely missed Mustafa's face.

The brothers tussled with each other until they ended up wrestling on the floor and making a wreck out of Rosetta's living room. They were at war, battling and trading blows like complete strangers.

It was Musa's sheer endurance and indomitable will that shifted the tide of the conflict. He was in an advantageous position, and mounted Mustafa and rained punches down on his face.

Blood splattered all over Mustafa's velour sweat suit. He could have overpowered Musa, but his speed made him a difficult opponent to tame.

Mustafa turned his back, withstanding every punch while he reached his hand between the cushions of the couch. He grabbed his .38 caliber revolver, swung it from the sofa and hit his brother with the butt of the gun. He turned the gun around, stood up and held Musa at gunpoint.

Their mother, Rosetta stomped into the living room. "God

damn it! What the hell are y'all doing? There's blood all over the floor and my new furniture!" she screamed at the top of her lungs. Her southern accent emphasized the intensity of her words. "Why the hell are you pulling a gun out on my son? That's your brother! And why is that thing in my house!" she continued.

"But Mom…" Mustafa stuttered.

"Don't but Mom me! Shit! I don't know what happened and I don't care. But you will not threaten the life of my first child! Yo' ass goes in and out of jail, and every time you come out, you cause bullshit! And you're gonna pull out a gun in my house? Get the fuck out!"

"But Mom…"

"Get out!"

Mustafa was frozen with confusion and disappointment. As angry as he was, he would not dare disrespect his mother so he quietly threw his jewelry on and tucked his gun into his waistband.

"If I see you again, I'm calling the police!" Rosetta warned.

Mustafa walked towards the door, embarrassed and with his head hung down in shame. He said, "Bye, Mom. Bye, Bro."

Musa looked his brother in the eyes and said, "You're not my brother!"

That was the last thing he said to his brother, and that was the last time he saw him in twenty years. A couple of months after their fight, Mustafa killed three men in an armed robbery that went awry, and one of the victims happened to be an undercover officer. He was caught and prosecuted to the fullest extent of the law.

******

A feeling of guilt lingered over Musa's head as he shuffled

around his old apartment. Those were memories that seemed to haunt him.

He was an older man with a heavy heart. The oldest and wisest son still couldn't manage to keep his little brother out of jail. And, he wasn't strong enough to keep the drugs away from Margie. Both his son and brother had been swallowed up by the system, and Margie, his first love, was lost in her addiction.

Musa paced back and forth in his lonely old apartment that resembled a battlefield of

paperwork. The apartment became a sort of purgatory where he housed all of his demons, and engaged in an eternal conflict with his conscience. The guilt weighed heavily on his shoulders, and although he could bring himself to forgive others, he could not forgive himself. Being the patriarch of his family and the oldest living male, he had an obligation to protect and educate all those that came after him. Sometimes a man's harshest judgements come from himself.

His lonely abode was a tomb built on self-loathing and disappointment. It was decorated with trophies and awards mixed into a stew of endless unrealized potential. He couldn't cure Margie's addiction, just like he couldn't deter his son and little brother from being in the streets.

As Musa moped around, he heated up his coffee and began sorting through his paperwork so that he could type his own deposition for court.

There was a sudden knock at his door. "Who is it?" he shouted.

"It's your son, Jamaal!"

Musa was startled as he walked to the door in his Fruit of the Loom briefs and slippers, and looked through the peephole.

Musa was always a very non-emotional individual, so much that he was considered to have borderline Asperger's Syndrome. Therefore, in spite of his excitement, he dampened his emotions.

When he opened the door, it was like a time warp. He was staring at a younger version of himself. Freedom stood there, looking young, strong, resilient and full of pride.

When Freedom saw his father, he had a good idea of what he might look like in about eighteen to twenty more years.

There they stood, face to face, mirror images of one another. Both men wore full beards. Freedom's was jet-black while Musa's was sprinkled with gray. Musa had maintained his athletic frame, but had a slight gut. They locked eyes, evaluating each other's stature. It was intimacy without touch or sound; only scent and sight.

Freedom could still remember the day his teenage body began to smell like his father's. He remembered how much his heart would beat to the point where it banged on his chest out of

sheer nervousness. For the first time in his life he saw his father, and it didn't cause anxiety. No, this time was different. It was an indescribable feeling of harmony that took over his being. He stretched his arms forward. In that moment his inner child screamed for paternal attention. He embraced his father and squeezed him while he whispered in his ear, "I'm sorry!"

"So am I, son! I'm sorry too."

Musa's response was reassuring and comforting. Their embrace was long and intense as tears of joy flooded their faces.

"Why didn't you come see me?" Freedom asked.

"Because I didn't want to see you like that."

"Like what?"

"Like a caged animal. It would have hurt too much."

"I understand."

"So, what are you going to do with your life now?" Musa asked his son. "You know that if you do the same thing, you'll get the exact same results."

"Nah, I ain't going back to the same way of living. I wrote a book, and I have a concept for a clothing line."

"Oh, okay. I like the idea of my son as an author. What's the book about?"

"It's sort of a self-help book; almost an up to date version of 'The Art of War', but more in laymen's terms. It outlines the basic tools of survival that assisted me throughout my years."

"Powerful. I like that. More young Black men need that kind of information. Good. You seem to be evolving."

"Pop?"

"Yes?"

"I just need some answers."

"You want to know why I was so hard on you and your mother? Well, I was young. I didn't know how to stop her from getting high. I couldn't control her. I just wanted us to be a normal family. I made a lot of sacrifices. I had scholarships to go to some of the best colleges in the country, but I chose Delaware State so that I could be close to my family. I had a temper problem, your mother had a drug problem, and the two don't mix."

"As for you, I was hard on you because you needed discipline. Think about it. You're a man now in your 30's, so you can understand. You have a child, right? As a child you were an unkempt, snot nosed asthmatic living in an environment that wasn't conducive to your development. It was frustrating, and I dealt with it in the wrong way. I apologize for you having to witness me and your

mother's altercations, but I do not apologize for disciplining you as
your father."

"Thanks."

"For what?"

"For apologizing. I forgive you, Dad. I'm a grown man now, and
I'm responsible for my life and my family. However, do you forgive
yourself?"

Musa paused and took a long hard look at his son. "No, it
torments me every day that my only son had been in federal prison
the past ten-plus years, and my first love is a crack head."

"You know, Mommy's clean now."

"Really?"

"Yeah. She came to visit me in the penitentiary. She looked really
good."

"*Alhamdulillah!* All praise due to Allah! Son, you have a second
chance at life. Allah has spared you. I named you Jamaal because it
means 'beauty'—not in the literal sense but in the spiritual sense.
You have the ability to lead. You are a talented and charismatic individual. Allah has blessed you with many great attributes. Now you
can abuse them by serving Satan, or you can take up the cause of
righteousness and do great positive work with your gifts."

After years of being estranged from one another, their once
broken bond was repaired. That little part of Freedom's heart,
the inner child that cried out for his father, was finally answered.
Through forgiveness, both men had lifted a burden off of their
shoulders, and opened the floodgates for them to show love to one
another again.

They spent the rest of the day catching up on old times. They ate fried fish from Famous Fish on 145th Street and St. Nicholas Avenue.

Musa agreed to edit Freedom's book for him, and assist with putting it out. Freedom titled his book, "The Morals and Dogma of Freedom". The book was meant to simplify higher metaphysical principles, and making the applications of such principles easier.

Freedom had become humble and spiritually connected with himself when he was locked away. He discerned that his true loves were writing and learning. He found his purpose. He wanted to be a catalyst for his own namesake.

Staring into his father's eyes was like staring at the universe. In his father he found the source of his flame and realized that his battle was not with the streets, the police or politicians. His battle was for clairvoyance and financial independence. Freedom, like his father, was to carry the torch and be a revolutionary fit for a new day and age, with futuristic means of combat.

With all these family reunions and spiritual awakenings, he still had the restless spirit of Hashish and Samaya lingering in the background of his cinematic thoughts.

CHAPTER 19

REVELATIONS

THERE was a storm brewing, and the storm was inside Freedom's heart. He had only been home for a short time, but he was beginning to get acclimated to society and all the changes, like cell phones, social media and the overall computer based culture of the new millennia.

He was focused on changing his circumstances, but before he could turn his back on his old lifestyle, he had to tie up all loose ends. That meant avenging Samaya and pulling Supreme and Pistola out of the life with him. However, he was uncertain about Supreme and some of his new acquaintances.

Freedom was slick enough to stay below the radar for a couple of months, but he was feeling antsy. Nefertarie had proven a perfect ally and spiritual guide.

He decided to call one street dude that he knew would never change. He met up with Pistola in downtown Brooklyn at Junior's. Freedom was sitting down stuffing his face when Pistola walked in. He spotted Freedom instantly and walked over to his table.

"Dimelo, Primo!"

The two men shook hands and exchanged hugs like two long lost siblings.

Before Pistola sat down he said, *"Mira,* Freedom. You looking like a bodybuilder. What the fuck was you doing?"

"Nothing, nigga. I see your English has gotten way better," Freedom said with a smirk.

"Yo, we need you out here, *papi.* Shit is getting crazy. Your man, Supreme is linked up wit' the *morenos* from Queens. Those motherfuckers are crazy; just fucking unprofessional."

"Are you serious?"

"Your boy, Supreme is a good dude, but he got a dangerous weakness for woman and that nose candy. Personally, I stay away from them. I come around when needed or when the price is right, feel me? So, when you go around them dudes, be careful. I can trust Supreme, but I just can't really trust them dudes around him."

"Wassup wit' Mercedes? How's she doing?" Freedom asked.

"Oh shit! You don't know?" Pistola's face saddened and took on a more somber expression.

"Well, what's up, God?"

"She's dead."

"What the fuck! Who killed her?"

Pistola paused for a moment, as though he didn't want to go into details. It hurt him to be the bearer of bad news.

Freedom leaned forward and pushed his piece of cheese cake to the side. His eyes were piercing and intense. "Pistola, tell me wassup. Don't leave me in the dark beloved!" he whispered.

"Okay. I don't know exactly what happened, but she got shot up by some Dominican cats."

Freedom's face shrank down to an angry scowl as one name echoed in his head and thundered through his mind; *"Sopa! That motherfucker!"*

"Oh, yeah, and Supreme was there."

Now Freedom was truly shocked. "What do you mean Supreme was there?"

"Listen, nobody knows exactly what happened, but word on the streets is that Mercedes tried to set him up with some O.G. Dominican shooters, but he got up out that shit."

"I don't understand."

"You understand. You're just in denial. Supreme was fucking your bitch. Everybody knew about it."

"Wow! So, I got to watch my own brother! I don't care that he fucked her. I'm just mad that he did it behind my back." Freedom put his head in his hands in frustration. "If he would hide that from me, he'd hide anything," he said.

Freedom had to come to terms with this twisted revelation. Both Samaya and Mercedes were murdered, and the one friend that he thought was loyal had betrayed him. He was all alone, with no one he could truly trust. But Pistola had proven himself to be unshakably loyal to him.

Freedom only had a week left in the halfway house. Pistola took the time to give Freedom a ride back there.

"Do me a favor, Pistola. Remember, you did not see me." He turned and looked at Pistola before he got out of the car and asked, "Are you with me? Can I depend on you? 'Cause you're all I got right now."

Pistola stared back at his mentor dead in the eyes and said, *"Sí, Primo.* I got you."

"Don't even fret. I got a plan. We're gonna be okay. We gotta get out of this shit. We can't do this forever."

"I'm content in doing what I am doing, papa," Pistola responded.

"You know where this shit ends, right?" Freedom asked. It was a cryptic warning that death could be right around the corner.

Pistola had never seen Freedom in a space where he is unsure or uncertain.

Freedom was uneasy. His money was getting low. Although he had solidified his family ties with his mother and father, he had yet to visit his daughter, Rain. He didn't know how to face her or if she'd forgive him. He couldn't forgive himself, and in his very soul he knew that despite the fact that someone else had killed her, ultimately, Samaya's blood was on his hands.

******

Freedom felt a chill as he crossed the street to return home. It was October, and the summer was dying. The dead of winter was steadfastly approaching. He despised going back to the halfway house, but Federal Probation left him no choice.

Two white men he had never seen before were standing in the lobby, eyeing him as he walked in. One was a tall, athletic younger guy who was obviously new. The other was an older, short, balding guy in his late 40's.

The shorter one spoke first while extending his hand. "Hi. You're Jamaal I presume. I'm Detective Berkowitz of the 103rd Precinct in Queens. We'd like to sit down with you and ask you a few questions."

Freedom's answer was short and direct. "No! Ain't shit for us to discuss unless y'all arrest me. Get the fuck outta my face!"

"Okay, tough guy. I guess you don't want to know who murdered your baby's mama!" Berkowitz said with a devious look while staring up at Freedom, who spun around instantly.

The second officer, Detective Matthews, broke the ice. "Why

don't we find a secluded room where we can all talk and discuss things in private?"

The three men entered a room and took seats around a small conference table.

Berkowitz initiated the discussion. "So, judging by your record, you're no stranger to being interrogated by the police. But honestly, what I want you to know is that I'm just doing my job, and I don't give a fuck who lives or dies as long as my family is okay."

"Now, about six months ago someone slaughtered your ex-girl-friend and her husband. When we did an investigation, we couldn't find anything on her or her husband's background that would have caused someone to break into their house and commit such a brutal murder."

"Then, we dug deeper into Samaya's past, and we found out that you were her drug dealing, thug ass baby daddy. So, we figured that whoever killed her was actually sending you a message."

Detective Matthews chimed in. "You must be in bed with some dangerous people." Then he passed Freedom a yellow folder full of crime scene photos. "So, do you have any idea who would want to send you this kind of message?"

Freedom opened the folder, and before he could flip through the pictures, the first one he saw was of Samaya's mutilated body parts. He almost threw up but held back his vomit.

"Whoever did this wasn't new at it. They were definitely profes-sionals, and it was meant to send you a message. Now, I know how this goes. You're thinking that now that you're out of the peniten-tiary you're going to get some type of revenge. Well, just know that we're watching," Berkowitz warned him.

Freedom put his head down, dropping the folder and its

contents. As tears streamed down his face, there was one name that kept flashing in his head: *"Sopa... Sopa... Sopa!"*

Matthews picked up the folder and placed his hand on Freedom's shoulder. "We can catch him. Just give us a chance. Drop a name."

Freedom slowly lifted his head and said, "Get the fuck out of here!"

Those crime scene photos were locked in his mind. The morbid, grueling images would never fade from his memory. Thought and imagination can be the servants of pain and agony. He tucked Samaya's memory away in a sweet, heavenly part of his heart, free from contamination and unsullied by the debauchery that was her brutal murder.

The detectives left their cards on the table in front of Freedom before they walked out.

Every man has his demons; his personal torments; his dark side. What happens when a man gets to a point where his demons take over; where he embraces his dark side; where he becomes everything he despises in himself; where he reaches his breaking point? Freedom was there, and there was only one name that was the focus of his hatred and vengeance. That name was Sopa!

CHAPTER 20

WELCOME BACK

IN a real old rent subsidized apartment with hardwood floors on Hillside Avenue in Jamaica, Queens, the fresh scent of Pine-Sol and bleach permeated the air. Umi had done her usual cooking and cleaning of the apartment before the arrival of her grandchildren.

She was a powerful, headstrong older woman, and a single mother. She grew up in the 70's when the streets had morals and principles.

Umi was typically high-spirited, but the loss of her daughter, Samaya kept her in mourning. Samaya was the eldest of her three children, and the only girl who had spent her childhood being a homemaker and watching over her younger siblings.

Umi was a devout Muslim woman who stuck to her traditional ideals. She was the stern matriarch of her family.

Samaya was the light of the family, and her death had traumatized all of them collectively. She was still adjusting to not having her daughter around.

On this particular day Umi was grooming her grandkids. Rain and her cousins were sitting on Umi's couch waiting to get their hair braided, when all of the sudden the phone rang. "Yes, hello," she answered.

"As-salamu alaykum."

"Wa-Alaikum salaam. I'm fine, but may I ask who is speaking?"

"This is Jamaal. I'd like to talk to Rain."

"Yes, you can. But I want you to know something, Jamaal," she spoke in a calm, firm and soothing manner. "Rain is your daughter, Jamaal. I'm an old woman. You are going to have to get your life together because your daughter needs you, and you need her."

"Is she available?" Freedom asked.

Reluctantly, Umi passed the phone to Rain.

"Hello" Rain was growing, and at fifteen years of age, she was having issues coping with the loss of her mother.

"Hey, Princess," he responded. "How's school?"

"It's okay." Rain's answers were short and emotionless, as though there was some underlying disgruntled energy in her voice. "Can I ask you something?" she continued.

"Sure. Shoot."

"Are you still in jail?"

"No, Princess. Daddy is free."

Like every little girl, her father was her first crush. Despite all the hardships, she still had a soft spot for her Dad.

After she let every one of her family members know that her father was free, she got back on the phone with him. "Do you know about what happened to Mommy?"

"Yes, babe. I know."

"I keep praying that Allah gives her back to us, but Umi says that Mommy is in Heaven now." Then she whispered, "I don't think there is a Heaven. I don't think there is a God."

"Why would you say that, Princess?"

"Because how come God always lets good people like Mommy die, and bad people like you live?"

"What makes me so bad?"

"'Cause you were in jail, and jail is for bad people," Rain answered.

Freedom could only grin at the brash, raw honesty of his young offspring. She was definitely Samaya's daughter; loving and sweet, yet brutally honest. "Rain, sometimes good people do bad things, you know."

"You mean like you?"

"Yes, like me."

"You coming to see me?"

"Yes, Princess. Now, let me speak to your grandma."

Umi loved Freedom like he was her own child, but she couldn't help but be infuriated by her daughter's murder. "You know, Rain needs you now more than ever, Jamaal. But I can't have her with you. I'd be worried for her safety."

"I know."

"Trust me, the average person would probably never allow you to set foot in your

daughter's life. Don't think everything is going to be peachy when you see her either. She's angry, and so am I. You're lucky I'm even letting you see her. But Allah says you can't deny a child their parent."

"I know. I think I'll come by to see her, and send some money soon. I just got to tie up some loose ends."

"No problem. But you can do me one favor. Avenge her, Jamal! You hear me? Those *kafirs* (infidels) cannot be allowed to live, Jamal!" Umi said, and slammed the phone down.

Freedom replayed Rain's echoes of torment in his head, contemplating her juvenile yet advanced revelation: *"If there is a God, why do bad things happen to good people?"*

Chapter 21

Redemption

FALL leaves were piled on the concrete pavement of downtown Brooklyn, creating a montage of nature versus modern man's dull shades of dirty gray concrete. The ground became a beautiful canvas for the leaves. All shades of brown, red and burnt orange with little splashes of green added a sort of Doomsday mystique.

Winter was lurking around the corner, and winter was a sign of death. In all indigenous cultures, this was the time that marked the end of the harvest. Summer is long gone, and Halloween is the time of demons, ghouls and goblins that are steadfast approaching. And with it, the city is going to be a cold and dangerous place at night.

******

Freedom had spent six months at the halfway house, and had fulfilled his obligation to federal parole. Being free from urinalysis tests and weekly check-in's, he craved two things: a good old blunt of weed, and two 10-milligrams of Percocet pain killers. He was never one to be addicted to narcotics, but he was an escapist. Reading, writing and drugs were his way of escape.

******

Elsewhere in Brooklyn, Nefertarie sat patiently on her porch next to the door of her salon. She was smoking on a joint packed with Kush. It was Freedom's last day on parole, and she knew that she was a big part of getting him through the whole ordeal.

Nefertarie had on a brown corduroy blazer with a white button-down shirt, fitted Gap denim jeans and a pair of cowboy boots to match. She was adorned with organic jewelry. Her bracelets, rings and necklaces were made from a combination of quartz and amethyst crystals, and copper and silver bangles. Her Asian eyes had a subtle blend of bronze, gold and brown eyeshadow that added highlights to her enchanting eyes.

In the past six months she and Freedom had grown very close to one another. She enjoyed guiding him through his journey as a student of African centered occult. She also organized his jail notes into a book and created a Word file for them. She admired his dedication to his family and his unquenchable thirst for knowledge.

As Freedom walked up the block with a confident stride, Nefertarie could spot him from a block away. He had perfect posture and walked with his chest out and a sturdy, almost regal stride.

"Peace, King!" she greeted.

"Peace, Queen!" Freedom responded.

Nefertarie always gave Freedom intense, soul-piercing eye contact.

"Did you finish typing the book?" he asked.

"Of course I did, Brother. There are still a couple of pages to edit." She handed him a stack of papers.

"Thank you so much. Now, we just got to find a good printer. You have any ideas?"

"Yes, I have plenty of ideas. Remember, my uncle wants us to clean up his money, and this book of yours could be a catalyst for much more."

"Okay, Sis. I'm excited. You know, I was thinking that it might be best to just self-publish my work instead of looking for a publisher."

"I think you're absolutely right. Let's put our heads together and figure it out. Are you okay, Freedom? I thought you'd be a little more enthusiastic now that you're free."

Freedom's eyes wandered and a strong look of uncertainty emulated from his aura. "It's just... nothing." As much as he wanted to keep a positive outlook on things, he couldn't. He was clearly at odds with Sopa, and he didn't have the cash or resources it would take to go to war.

"I sense something. I see something in your eyes. Come inside. Let's talk," Nefertarie said, and led him upstairs to her apartment above the salon.

Once inside, Freedom was taken aback by the multitude of statues and candles that were all over the apartment. There was a pungent aroma of patchouli oil permeating through the air.

Nefertarie directed him to sit down on her black leather couch while she walked around her home, lighting oil burners and wickers.

Freedom scanned the room, gazing at the many different altars and spiritual sigils. One particular item in the corner drew his attention. It was a small wooden table with a human skull replica made of glass on it. Next to it sat a lit, tall black candle and a wooden bowl of roasted peanuts. There was also a large bottle of Devil's Springs over-proof liquor. Something about that altar seemed surreal and threatening at the same time. Time seemed to stand still, and Freedom began to fall into a sort of trance while watching the flickering wick of the candle flame. He felt an instant heat rise in his body and wanted to leave.

For the first time in his life, he was scared. There were so many intense emotions soaring about inside him. The dimly-lit room filled with mystic items seemed to heighten the anxiety coursing within him.

Then his eyes wandered over to a poster on the door of an inverted five-pointed star with the head of a goat inside it, and in that moment he considered that Nefertarie might be a devil-worshiping harlot; a black widow entangling him in her web.

Although every part of Freedom's mind told him to escape, his curiosity surpassed his urge to leave. So, against his better judgement, he stood up to take a closer look.

Under the goat's head were words that read, "Do As Thou Wilst". He repeated the words over and over, attempting to find their meaning. He didn't want to continue snooping around, so he sat back down. But his eyes could not avoid the sight of that black candle and crystal skull.

Then a gentle caress came across the side of his face. Samaya was sitting right next to him. She rested her hand on his lap and said, "Jamaal, I forgive you. I love you... I love you..."

As tears streamed down Freedom's face, he felt a serenity in the depths of his heart. "I'm so sorry! I'm so—"

Samaya responded, "It's okay. It's okay. Wake up!"

Freedom's eyes snapped open, and he found Nefertarie cradling his head in her arms, and telling him, "It's okay, Freedom. You dozed off. When I came back in the room you were talking in your sleep. I don't bring many people up here, and no one ever falls asleep here. You must have felt comfortable." She grinned.

Freedom sat up. "Nah, I think I just got so much shit on my mind that I just fell asleep." As his eyes scanned the room, everything was exactly the same as it was in his dream, except that none of the candles were lit. "What is that skull for? I hope you ain't on no devil shit," he commented.

"No, baby. That skull is your indigenous science. That altar is for Baron Samedi. That is you, my love. You have nothing to fear from that, and in due time I will teach you much more."

Freedom didn't know why he trusted her. Maybe part of it was because of Money Mike; but more so it was because he was extremely intrigued. There was clearly some sort of sexual tension between them.

Nefertarie sat across from him, resembling an ebony enchantress. Her slanted eyes seemed to end where her cheek bones began. The diamond stud in her nose and the silk scarf that wrapped her forehead gave her an almost Gypsy-like appearance, while her curly, jet-black locks draped down the sides of her head. He liked her, but her wisdom made him feel bashful; almost childlike in her presence.

"Can I ask you a serious question, Freedom?" Her voice was melodic yet strong, with a hint of a Dionne Warwick-like baritone.

"Yes, you can."

"Where are you going to live now that you're out of the halfway house… honestly?"

"Um, I'm not sure. Shit is kinda crazy for me, so I really don't know. But I'll figure something out."

"Well, here. Take this. You're free to come over any time you need to," Nefertarie said, and passed him a copy of her keys.

"Are you sure? I mean, don't you have a man?"

She grinned and said, "No, it's not like I'm suggesting we're in a relationship. I just think that you need someone to have your back right now. You're about to enter into an intense time in your life. Actually, I really wish you wouldn't do anything but invest all your time into the amazing little book of proverbs that you wrote.

But I know what you're going through is ultimately necessary to complete your transformation."

"What do you mean?"

"I mean that you have enemies who want to extinguish your fire, and we're not going to let that happen. Will you promise me something, Freedom?"

"Yes."

"I need you to trust me like you trust my uncle. Will you trust me?"

Freedom hung his head down in doubt. He didn't answer because he could not commit to simply trusting on blind faith. "I'll try, Nefertarie. I'll try."

In that moment, they solidified an ecclesiastical bond between "the witch" and "the warrior".

CHAPTER 22

IT WAS ALL SO SIMPLE

THE streets of Jamaica, Queens were an inferno on Earth. The last stop on the E-train is sort of a crossroads and a small melting pot of Caribbean and African culture.

Right near the train station it was a festive night, and luxury cars littered the block. Some of the noise and constant commotion was caused by rush hour Jamaican van drivers advertising their route numbers by yelling, "Number four!" "Number Five!" "Number t'ree!"

Jamaica, Queens had birthed legendary hip-hop artists such as Run DMC, 50 Cent, LL Cool J, and Nicki Minaj, and even gave birth to the late, great singer, Billie Holiday.

Just as much as the area is noted for its contribution to music, it can equally be recognized for its addition to New York's criminal underworld, like the "original" Supreme, who rose to power as a drug lord in the late 80's and early 90's, and even Chaz, the now reformed bank robber.

One of the Big Apple's biggest contradictions is Queens, where the crime rate escalates despite being two miles away from Trump real estate. Many have been fooled by this ghetto with pockets of illusionary suburbs. The truth is that no one was safe anywhere.

Why? Because of systemized attacks that afflict low income areas internationally.

Despite all its contradictions, Jamaica, Queens is still an epicenter for Black culture. What's more is that Jamaica has proven to be a beacon for wealthy, progressive African Americans, so much so that it rivals Harlem's legendary status, which made people coin the phrase, "Queens gets the money".

******

Supreme stood outside of the Dunkin' Donuts on Parsons and Archer with all of his comrades. He was the head of a legion of beasts. Much like the mythological Leviathan, PNA, Money Gang and Kitty Gang were all tentacles of a much larger animal.

All of the PNA and Kitty Gang boys were scheduled to perform at Perfections Strip Club.

Joka rocked back and forth while his song, "Trappin' N Rappin'" blared out of Sef's speakers.

Supreme always wore the best and latest fashions. He was pacing back and forth while staring down at his cell phone and smoking a cigarette. He was anxious to see his blood brother.

Freedom had finally revealed himself to Supreme with a phone call, and was instantly ordered to come to Queens in a cab. In Supreme's true fashion of being a very jovial, flamboyant brother, he told Freedom to be prepared to have a lot of fun.

But one person's idea of fun could easily be another's source of torture and torment. For example, while a lot of people enjoyed strip clubs with semi-nude women frolicking around, some might be repulsed by his or her sisters being exploited in such a misogynistic manner, and resent certain stereotypes perpetuated by society.

As much as Freedom enjoyed and celebrated the image of woman, he would have preferred a more intimate setting.

He had to reunite with his only childhood friend. Their bond was forged in adolescence. Together they shared in losses and triumphs, and dark secrets, like the killing of Fire, the third member of their childhood trio. It was just an unspoken truth that neither of them ever mentioned.

Fire was a casualty of war. It wasn't about whether he acted out against them or not. He died because he was with the adversary. They had no choice, and with the amount of blood on their hands, Fire's ghost could not find the room to haunt them. They both suffered from restless nights, wrestling with their consciences. So, there was always a sense of unwavering loyalty, which Supreme had violated in a way by having had relations with Mercedes.

Freedom was skeptical about Supreme. The love was there, but they had grown apart during the past ten-plus years. They had become grown men who had evolved in their own individual ways; settled in their ways; and were resolved in their views, but still sharing a common goal; wealth, property and financial freedom.

Freedom got out of the cab on the corner of Jamaica Avenue and Parsons Boulevard while on his cell phone talking to Supreme.

"Ayo, God. Where are you at, beloved? I just got out the cab. I'm over here by this movie theater shit."

"Okay, yeah, God. I see you, son! I see you!"

When they met up, they locked arms like two long lost, war torn comrades, and embraced one another.

Supreme stood back. "Look at my bro! Yo, God, you got big like me. How many pullups you do in a set, nigga?" he asked.

"I'm putting up like fifteen pullups on my first set, then I can burn out on ten a set."

"That's cool. I'm still putting up like twenty a set, nigga." Supreme jumped up and did a quick twenty pullups on the stoplight.

The two shared some laughs as Supreme took Freedom around and introduced him to the fellas. But despite the jubilant atmosphere, there was something uneasy in the air.

Freedom was uncomfortable, and despite all the sour diesel and Percocet's in his system, he couldn't ignore the obvious. He questioned himself mentally. The paranoia could be a side effect of the weed. Maybe he didn't have the same drug tolerance after all the years of sobriety. He had spent a long time confined. The street lights, honking horns and the overall noise of city life confused him. *Is this really home? This couldn't be where I belong,* he thought silently to himself.

Supreme was drunk out of his mind. He was the loudest, flyest guy on the block, sporting a brown wool Polo sweater with brown suede elbow patches, the latest Polo boots to match, and new school Gazel shades.

It was a new era for them both, but Freedom was still stuck in a time warp. He watched everyone's movements around him while gathering intel. He paid attention to their Jamaican accents, and watched himself around them because some beefs do not die easily. His mind was like a computer, inputting all the data.

He watched all of Supreme's associates, especially Gun Smoke and GL. They were dangerous, and he knew it. At least GL could be spoken to. His mind was moldable to some degree.

Gun Smoke, on the other hand, had no cares whatsoever, and was a wild card.

Automatically, the wheels began turning in Freedom's head. He knew that he had to assimilate into this new hierarchy. He kept a close eye on the van drivers who seemed to be oblivious to all the hoopla and remained self-contained in a vacuum of their own urban drama.

"Yo, 'Preme! Wassup, God? What are we waiting for? Why are we standing out here?" Freedom asked.

"We're waiting for my man, Kendu. 'Member I told you about him?"

"You mean the dude you claim is your right-hand man now?"

"Why you hating? He's a good nigga, man. I fucks wit' him hard-body, and he's riding wit' a nigga, you heard? Money Gang!"

"Okay, Money Gang. I get it, nigga. You can trust these niggas, 'cause I don't."

Suddenly, a brand new 2012 black Range Rover drove around the corner in reverse with a 250 lb. chunky, light-skinned man holding onto the hood. He appeared to be arguing with his girlfriend who was driving the car and screaming at him from the driver's seat.

"Get the fuck off the car with your nasty ass! Go drive that ugly bitch's car! Oh, I forgot! She ain't got no car, you fucking piece of shit! Come get your friend, Supreme!" the girl yelled.

Supreme quickly spun away from Freedom and jumped in between the feuding couple.

Kendu and Stacey were always going through conflict. They were a toxic mix. She was a bipolar cocaine addict, while he was a charismatic yet violent bruiser with a severe temper. He was the type that never shot a man in his life, but has choked and beat a couple of people to death.

Stacey stopped the car, got out and swung a Remy Martin Red bottle at Kendu, all in one motion.

Supreme managed to deflect the bottle, but it did not stop Kendu from hitting Stacey with a slap that sent her careening to the ground.

Stacey was a light-skinned girl of biracial parents. She bruised easily. She jumped up from the ground like a woman possessed.

Supreme struggled with both of them, trying to diffuse the situation while everyone around pulled out their camera phones to record the shenanigans.

All this commotion was making Freedom very antsy. He shrank into himself, placed his back against the wall while watching the street and preparing himself for anything. He was nervous, and unfortunately the liquor and drugs put him in a complete state of paranoia.

Supreme walked over with Kendu next to him, while Stacey hopped back into her jeep and sped off, all the while cursing Kendu out.

"Man, that bitch is lucky I didn't clap her ass!" Kendu said while tapping his waist reassuringly.

Supreme and Freedom knew that he was carrying a gun.

"So, what up, niggas? I heard a lot about you," Kendu continued, referring to Freedom.

Freedom wasn't the type to get too familiar too fast, and from what he saw thus far, he didn't like Kendu. "Yeah, I heard some things about you too. But if you're 'Preme's brother, then you're my brother," he responded.

"You ready to work and get this paper?" Kendu asked.

"I ain't no worker."

"Pardon me, my nigga! Yo, Supreme, ya man type sensitive,

man," Kendu said with a grin and laughed a little before speaking again. "My nigga, I wasn't calling you a worker, but this here is Money Gang, ya heard? So, I need to know if you're ready to put in work."

The tension in the air was thicker than cold cooked grits, so Supreme quickly intervened, putting his hands on both men's shoulders. "Tonight is a celebration night. Let's all talk business another time, okay?"

Freedom and Kendu's personalities clashed. Both men felt equally entitled to that number one spot. While Freedom had practically been his life-long friend and ally, Kendu had been Supreme's right-hand man for the past decade. But he lacked the calm calculated reserve, and was more of a spontaneous risk taker. All of this added up to the fact that they were polar opposites.

Freedom made it is priority to stay vigilant. His senses were picking up on something as Supreme began to round up all the fellas.

There were two gay looking crossdressers walking past. No one looked them in the face, and in an almost homophobic sense, they completely ignored them.

Then all of the sudden, two Nissan Altima's swerved onto Archer Avenue and made an illegal right turn on Parson's Boulevard, which caught the attention of everyone on the block. Both Altima's came to an abrupt stop.

Elmo clutched his .45 caliber handgun through the pocket of his Pelle Pelle Soda Club leather.

When the two windows rolled down, Freedom locked eyes with the passenger. They didn't recognize one another, but the voice was familiar to Freedom. It was Magnum.

"Aye, pussy, kill my nephew and t'inks ya can walk 'round? Ya dead, pussy! Ya dead!"

Everyone moved towards the vehicles to rush the passengers while Freedom stood back, anticipating the worst. He knew that the worst thing he could do is run up to a car with tinted windows.

Before anyone could reach the Altima's, the two crossdressers off to the side and out of everyone's peripheral vision pulled out Mac-11 submachine guns capable of releasing 32 bullets in less than two seconds. It was an elaborate ambush. No one had time to think.

Elmo turned around and opened fire while rushing to give Supreme some cover.

Freedom got as low as possible while running through the crowd and pulling Kendu out of the way. They both took cover behind a dollar van while in clear view of the Altima's. "Give me ya gun!" Freedom shouted at Kendu.

"Okay, ya gotta do something wit' it!" he yelled to Freedom.

Freedom looked up and locked eyes with Magnum again. In that single instant—in that brief nanosecond—time paused and they recognized one another. Their minds floated to the past; to a softer, calmer, simpler time. And as though they were in some euphoric dream interrupted by this nightmare called life, they were forced to leave the past and return to the present when the driver screamed, "Magnum, shoot da bwoy now!"

Both Freedom and Magnum came back to reality and opened fire, but something made them avoid shooting each other. Instead, they shot in each other's direction, realizing that this war was much more personal than either of them knew.

Each of the two crossdressing assassins jumped into the back seat of either car, and the Altima's sped off, while everyone else had scattered off into their own direction to avoid police contact.

Freedom jumped into the passenger seat of Supreme's jeep.

"Yo, Free, you good?" Supreme asked.

"Yeah, I'm straight," he responded and checked his body for bullet wounds.

Unfortunately—or better yet fortunately—they were accustomed a violent lifestyle and threatening situations. Certain behaviors became protocol. The first move is to get to safety, then came damage control and a casualty count.

Supreme checked in with Elmo and the rest of Money Gang, PNA and Kitty Gang via cell phone. "Yo, Kendu, no casualties. Everybody's good, so we're good."

"Take me to Brooklyn now," Freedom said to Supreme.

"Fuck you mean, Brooklyn? We're going to Club Perfection to party, God!"

"I ain't with this shit, man. We almost had a fucking hit done on us and you talking 'bout partying? Are you fucking serious nigga?"

Kendu intervened. "Yo, 'Preme, ya man's on point, fam. He saved my life for real. We gotta keep this nigga gripped up."

"It was nothing, man. Just doing what I would want done for me. Yo, 'Preme, this ain't smart. We should be planning our next move," Freedom said.

"You're always wit' that planning shit. I don't plan; I just hustle, nigga. Fuck them Jamaican niggas! That shit's some regular shit. Niggas is salty over how we manhandled their little man, that's all. Trust me, I'm getting all them niggas hit!"

"That's exactly what I'm saying. This is different. That was Magnum in that car. The nigga was talking about Fire, man. Those are them Deadly Lion niggas."

"Aw, that old shit with the nigga, Fire. Now we gotta assume that all those motherfuckers are together."

"No, that's how you made that mistake last time."

Supreme became enraged and sped up to 110 mph on the highway. "Don't bring that shit up! That was me holding you down! Now you regret it? You forgot what them niggas tried to do to Samaya?"

There was a nonverbal agreement to silently pause in the conversation. The very idea of Samaya brought a powerful emotion.

"You know what, Freedom? You're built for this shit, man. We didn't choose this life; it chose us. We're gonna get all those motherfuckers one by one. But right now, we're gonna have some fun!" Supreme said as he stopped at the light. He took out a rolled up dollar bill and took two snorts of cocaine before passing it back to Kendu.

Freedom wasn't shocked; he was appalled. He was no one to judge, but he felt that cocaine was too hard of a drug.

Within less than a few hours being around Supreme's operation, he saw the holes in the foundation. With excessive drug use comes impaired judgement, and with impaired judgement comes detrimental mistakes that could lead to being confined to a cell or a coffin. Freedom was at a crossroad.

The rest of the night sort of played out in front of his eyes like a bad music video starring him. Everyone laughed, joked and slapped the asses of sexy, voluptuous women as they danced around.

Freedom did enjoy watching the PNA boys perform on stage. It was actually the highlight of the entire night. The young guys had potential. It was the kind of potential that could take brothers from the block to the boardroom.

Perfections Night Club in Woodside, Queens was famous for its celebrity guests and exotic strippers. Ballers, gangsters, entertainers and your average Joe could all meet at the place and equally enjoy the festivities.

However, the defining moment is when the real moneymakers start throwing cash at the ladies. Many times rappers get paid to attend strip clubs and are given money to throw at the strippers.

Supreme was flamboyant by nature, and he felt like it didn't matter who was there. They wouldn't do it bigger than him. He ordered bottle after bottle of Rose Moët & Chandon Champagne. Everyone in the crew had their own bottle. "No cups, just bottles and buckets of ice! Money Gang, nigga!" he shouted.

Their table was surrounded by sultry, seductive vixens all gyrating to the rhythmic sounds of DJ Oso. You could not judge these women. They were hustlers too. They could smell the money, and they hunted for it, scouring the crowd of thirsty, lustful onlookers. They must be keen enough to spot the one whose loins will lead him to part with excessive amounts of cash to chase a sensual fantasy.

It all becomes intoxicating. The liquor, the flashing fluorescent lights and beautiful women clad in decorative G-strings, high heel boots and sparkling scented lotion that made them appear almost goddess-like.

One Coke bottle shaped dancer took notice of Freedom and slithered her way over to him. She mounted him in his seat and straddled him like a wild stallion. She wound her waist to the rhythm like a veiled belly dancer, serenading his snake until it rose to attention. Her name was Kesha a.k.a. Slim Goody.

"I don't have any money for you," Freedom said in her ear.

"So, I don't care. It's not always about money," she responded.

When Supreme saw this rare anomaly where his best friend was actually having fun, he had to make an event of it by showering the stripper with loads of cash.

Slim Goody then jumped into action by doing handstands and splits at the same time, and multiple gymnastic feats while keeping the moves very sexual. She had a tattoo on each butt cheek; a red stop sign on one and a green go sign on the other. She would make each cheek jump together and separately while synchronized with the music. Her body was tall and slender, yet shapely. She had a soft, heart-shaped butt and small breasts. She was naturally beautiful, but she masked it under makeup. She wore hazel contact lenses and had a long Brazilian weave.

She and Freedom were victims of the same lifestyle. As she swerved and swayed her pain away, putting her body on display and sacrificing her flesh for the luxuries that money could buy, he accepted her talent and let go of judgement, and for a solitary second he allowed himself to be lighthearted. He let go of the stress that haunted the earlier part of the night and let himself be momentarily whisked away to a paradise where it rained money, every faucet pumped champagne, and all the women were naked.

CHAPTER 23

FIRST LIGHT

THEY stumbled out of their vehicles and proceeded to check into the Marriott on 165th Street and Hillside Avenue.

Freedom and Supreme paired off with four voluptuous strippers they hijacked from Club Perfections. They were all super high and drunk. Once in their room everyone began undressing.

There was Slim Goody, a slender woman with a flat chest, huge buttocks, and full sensual pink lips. Her bangs hung perfectly over her forehead, and her light brown eyes flirtatiously gazed from under them. She had a crush on Freedom, and when she heard that he had just returned from prison, she wanted that "fresh home dick" as some women would say. Not only did she want to give him a treat, she decided to bring her friend, Apache.

Apache was a completely different animal. She was 5'5", thick and chocolatey. Her calf muscles bulged through the straps of her designer stilettoes. Her butt was firm and thick, and her beautiful full lips only added to her pearly white teeth, making her smile all too genuine and pure for a woman in her profession. When she walked, her stature alone shook the floor.

"Ahh shit, nigga! It's going down!" said Supreme while he kicked off his sneakers and dropped his pants. He had two Puerto Rican strippers with him; Star and Pebbles.

Pebbles stood on top of the bed winding her hips, while Star got on her knees and began to slowly suck Supreme's penis.

Supreme nodded at Freedom and said, "Now this is the life, nigga! You want some of this?"

Freedom grinned and bashfully rushed into the bathroom. He took a moment to himself. He had been ignoring Nefertarie's calls. It was late, and she was obviously worried about him. They weren't in a relationship; they were just close friends. But there was something else there. Despite how tantalizing and sexual the strippers were, something in his conscience told him that it wasn't right.

Freedom hadn't had intercourse in a long time. He sat in the bathroom, playing a mental recording in his mind, reflecting on everything that had happened that night. He questioned himself, wondering if he had lost his edge, and whether he was still made for that lifestyle of fast money, fast cars and even faster broads.

Then, all at once his thoughts mixed with his intoxication came crashing down. Paranoia, distrust and betrayal had set in. He was angry with Supreme. He didn't know where to place it. Of all the women in the world, why did Supreme have to have Mercedes? Supreme wasn't the same. The money and the power had gone to his head. He wasn't the same person that Freedom knew from before.

The walls were closing in on Freedom. He needed time to think, speculate and strategize.

Supreme yelled as he banged on the bathroom door, "Nigga, you okay? You taking a number 2,000 or something, God?"

Freedom responded, "Nah, I'm coming out right now." When he exited the bathroom there was a pile of coke on the coffee table, and the pungent scent of sour diesel weed permeated throughout the hotel room. He turned to Supreme and said, "Yo, God, I'm out!"

"Fuck you mean, you out? Fuck is you bouncing on me for?"

Freedom reluctantly answered, "Nah, it ain't nothing. I just got to hurry up and get back to the crib."

"A'ight, cool. That's kinda fucked up, but it's cool. I'll call you a cab."

The seeds of distrust had been sown.

******

Elsewhere, Narcotics Detective Sebastian Boyce from the 103rd Precinct sat in his parked car on 165th Street and Hillside Avenue with his partner, Detective Carlos Rivera.

"You know, this Supreme kid thinks he's the second coming of Supreme McGriffin, but he's not. He's just another pants sagging punk. You know this fuck has been filing complaints on me for harassment?"

"Are you shittin' me, Sebastian?"

"No. I know the fucker is up to no good. I just can't catch him. That piece of shit is responsible for several murders in the past five years, and he's never gotten the justice he deserves."

"Slick bastard!" Rivera exclaimed.

"Not slick; lucky and rich. He throws a lot of money around. I know he's been bribing a couple of officers at the precinct."

"Yeah, the fucker has a shootout, and then gets to party at a fucking hotel all night. He's living like a rock star."

"Shootout? What the fuck are you talking about, Rivera?"

"There was a shootout earlier by the train station."

"Okay, but how do you know this fucker was involved?"

"I got my sources, Seb."

"If that's the case, we need to shake the motherfucker down as soon as he leaves the hotel."

******

Freedom exited the hotel and quickly hopped into a cab.

******

"Seb, you ever see that guy?" Rivera asked, pointing at Freedom before he entered the cab.

"No, but he did go in with Supreme. They seemed pretty close. Find out who he is, since you have so many sources."

******

Sabastian was obsessed with his job to the point of using excessive force. His level of brutality gave him a bad reputation throughout the Jamaica, Queens community. Unfortunately but every so often a bad relationship with the community negates a good relationship with the precinct and a lot of other officers

Policing for over twenty years, he'd seen his fair share of corruption and injustice. Never one to take a payoff or pocket any drug money, he would have been considered what you call a good honest cop... maybe honest, but good? Absolutely not!

Sebastian Boyce was an Irish orphan raised by American parents. His history, however, was one of a street fighter. His specialty was Muay Thai and kick boxing. He considered himself a noble warrior who was loyal to the ancient Bushido code of the Samurai. The ideals and principles he acquired from studying martial arts accompanied him into the police force.

From early in his career he set a standard to never go after the small fry. Boyce preferred looking for what he considered the "real criminals". This determination and vigorous work ethic led to him being promoted to detective in just a two year span. He was an integral part of 103rd Precinct's Tactical Narcotics Team. He could have easily gotten a desk job or been promoted to sergeant or captain, but he preferred to stay a detective for over a decade. Why? Because he loved the grunt work. For Detective Boyce, nothing was more thrilling than stalking, catching and jailing his prey.

Sebastian Boyce stood 6'3", had a clean shaven head and white whiskers. His arms were covered with tattoos of dragons and skulls, and on one of his hands was a tattoo that read "F.T.W." which is an acronym for "Fuck the World". His motto was: *"I don't hate black people; I hate all people!"*

Now Detective Carlos Rivera was a short bodybuilder type. He hardly had ten years on the job, and he was a glory chaser. He wanted the fame and glory of being a hero.

Rivera quickly rose through the ranks after being shot while on duty thwarting a corner store robbery. He was a firm believer that social injustice can be cured from the inside out, so what better way to change the police department than to become a police officer?

The unlikely pairing of these two detectives was symbiotic in nature. For Rivera, his connection with his new partner gave him prestige and an infinite supply of martial wisdom; while Detective Boyce needed Rivera, who was someone that understood the culture of the neighborhood.

CHAPTER 24

ERZULIE DANTOR

FREEDOM slowly put his key in Nefertarie's apartment door. He was trying to be as stealthy as possible, but to no avail. His covert entrance was greeted by a three pound Buddha statue careening towards his head. Instinctively he knocked it away by blocking it with his forearm. The ceramic Buddha shattered on the floor.

Nefertarie was erupting with emotions. All night she had sat on her knees with her hands folded in prayer. Her long, thick jet-black locks draped to the floor, halfway covering her face. She was wearing nothing but her panties and housecoat while she rocked back and forth, worrying about Freedom all night.

"What the fuck is wrong with you?" Freedom yelled.

"Where the fuck were you all night?" she countered.

"Hold the fuck up, Nefertarie! Is this business or personal? We're not in a relationship!"

"You're right! We're not in a relationship! But dat don't mean I ain't gonna worry about you!" Enraged, she swung and hurt her hand while trying to land a significant punch on Freedom.

"Yo! Calm the fuck down! Why the fuck you keep trying to hit me?" Freedom asked.

"Because someone tried to kill you last night! You could have died! I thought you were dead!"

"How do you know that?" he asked, taken aback by her vision.

"I can't tell you. I just knew that someone tried to hurt you last night. I didn't want you to go, but I knew you had to see your friend. You two needed some closure."

"What do you mean?"

Nefertarie gently grabbed his hand and led him to the couch. She then pulled out her laptop. "What I mean is this." She pointed to a word document file on the screen and opened it up. It was entitled "Morals and Dogma of Freedom". It was a compilation of his philosophies and ideas organized into book form. "Aside from praying over your ass, I put some of your writings together from all those loose papers you had while in jail. Babe, you're a really talented writer. Don't stop. I know you and my uncle have business, but you don't need to be in the streets. And those friends you were with last night, they're no good for you, King."

"Listen. I appreciate you and everything that you have done for me thus far, but I know how to conduct myself. I know what I have to do. As a matter of fact, let me get my shit," Freedom said. He turned away and went to the back room to pack his stuff. He didn't know what he was doing. He was still intoxicated, out of his mind, and exhausted from a long night. He didn't respond to her reasoning. Instead, the heat from her inflammatory attitude had sparked an aggressive response.

"So now you're leaving? What good is that going to do? What the hell is wrong with you?"

Nothing was wrong with Freedom, but nothing was right either. His world was collapsing down on him all at once. He wasn't going to leave to hurt her; he was leaving to protect her. "This life I live is not for you. I don't want you worrying and praying for me. It's not fair to you."

After a brief pause, he put his head down while raising his eyes in a solemn fashion. "I don't want anything to happen to you... I don't want anything to happen to you..." he stuttered, "Like Samaya!" The anger, range and guilt were like shackles around his skull. Every other thought revolved around Samaya and his revenge.

Nefertarie was telepathic. She spoke in a calming tone while staring deep into his eyes. "I would tell you not to do it, but I know that would just push you away."

"Not to do what?"

"Find and kill Sopa."

Sometimes silence has a sound. It's an internal heartbeat; an altered state of being. They spoke through the silence.

Nefertarie's eyes were dreamy. Her mere glance could stop a person in their tracks. Her slanted, pearl-like eyes seemed to dance with the flickering candle lit room. She placed her hands gently on Freedom's face. "You have other allies on your side besides the ones you were with."

At that moment he thought of Pistola. He had to link up with him.

"I fear that if you follow your friends, you will find your death," she continued.

From that moment, Freedom began to look at her in depth. She was his guardian angel, and he felt as though an insatiable flame had gathered at the base of his stomach. This was more than a young woman giving guidance to a young man. This was love. Not necessarily sexual, but more intense. It was spiritual.

Nefertarie was like the manifestation of the mythological Medusa. Yet where the myth said that her appearance turned men to stone, in her case it was the opposite. Her stunning beauty invigoratingly enchanted the souls of a men. Her locks were like snakes and her eyes were fire. Her voice echoed with the passion of a queen.

Freedom stood in front of her resembling an African warrior preparing for a splendid mating dance.

It was early in the morning with a fiery bluish-orange sunrise. Beams of light crept into the dark apartment through the blinds.

Their union was highly unlikely. They hardly knew one another, and yet it was as though they had been friends for eternity. Simultaneously they threw caution and reason to the wind, giving into one of the strongest primordial forces known to man.

Before another word could have been uttered, Freedom's strong chiseled arms wrapped around Nefertarie's waist and pulled her in. Her soft pink lips pressed firmly against his own. Sensual kisses showered her neck, and he slowly worked his way down to her ears as her heart began to race. He whispered, "I thought about you all night. I can't get you off my mind."

Goosebumps rose all over her body, and she became more and more aroused with each and every lick. It was as though he was worshiping her as a Black goddess.

He was firm yet delicate while turning her around and pressing her breasts against the wall. Pulling her housecoat off, he slowly ran his tongue down her neck and back to the base of her spine.

Nervously she cringed as all the heat in her body rushed to her vagina.

Then he softly commenced to licking the inner walls of her ass. She arched her back, pushing it out even more, and he answered by increasing the intensity. "Turn around!" he commanded. He lifted her off the ground and she wrapped her thick chocolatey legs around his waist. He carried her to the couch and laid her on her back.

"I love you, Freedom! I love you!" she muttered.

Quickly he took off his clothes, revealing his well-sculpted abs and firm muscular chest.

She stared at him in awe and motioned him to mount her. He shook his head no, and shoved his throbbing dark rod in her face. He wrapped his arms around her waist and lifted her into a standing sixty-nine position. With her thighs resting on his shoulders, he licked her sweet, pink, pearly clitoris with his tongue, flicking it up and down until her sweet juices flooded between her legs.

Nefertarie responded by softly kissing and teasing his staff before she placed the head into her mouth. Her mouth was hot and wet, and she soft-stroked him with her tongue. Then she rhythmically swallowed it to the base of his scrotum and deep-throated him without gagging. Her head moved to a silent beat, and before he could explode he placed her back on the leather couch.

Wasting no time, he placed the tip of his rock-hard Johnson inside her. He angled himself, rubbing the rim of his penis on her pelvic bone area. Each stroke brought them closer and closer to climax. "Cum for me, baby!" he said as he leaned back and licked his thumb. Producing multiple stimuli, he thrust and rotated his pole around while working her clitoris with his finger.

Nefertarie could feel his heart racing as beads of sweat trickled down his face. Her ecstasy was peaking. She gyrated faster and faster, and at that very moment they both reached their zenith. She screamed in absolute nirvana as she had an orgasm.

Freedom was about to erupt with his semen. She wrapped her

legs around him tighter, grabbed his round shapely butt and pulled him inside of her. He let out a deep grunt.

Nefertarie's legs trembled uncontrollably as he softly pecked her neck. She continued to have multiple orgasms. Tears of joy began to stream from her eyes. She stared into the black abyss of her lover's eyes. "Freedom, I love you. You ain't leaving me."

CHAPTER 25

JUDAS

"...How would you feel if you woke up one morning and saw an M-16 muzzle at your jaw?
Feel like you wanna disappear, but you can't..."

THE song "Murderer" by Bounty Killa was one of Don-Don's favorite songs He sat in his office awaiting the arrival of Kendu. Earlier on he gave him a call. Cutting off their coke supply was a strategic move that could backfire.

The assassination attempt that took place on Parsons and Archer was a complete failure, so they decided to methodically pick them off one by one.

Kendu had no idea what Don-Don wanted with him, but the idea of betrayal never crossed his mind. He'd been working with Don-Don for years. In fact, his relationship to his coke connection was deeper than his love for Supreme. So, being that he was instructed to come alone, he knew that this was a special business meeting.

Kendu walked into the salon with the style of a true pimp. He was an old school dude who prided himself on being classy. He kept his hands and feet nicely manicured, with a long pinky nail for sniffing. He was adorned in gold and diamond jewelry like a urban pharaoh, with bronze and wood framed Cartier shades to match. His bowlegged limp only added to his Mac Daddy persona. He complimented the ladies on their hair and shoes, lighting up the salon with blushing and giggling women in admiration.

By the sound of the music blaring out of the office, it was obvious that Don-Don was inside so Kendu walked in.

"What did I tell you about knocking before you enter? That's an easy way to get shot! Now, lock the door behind you and sit down," Don-Don said, and sucked his teeth.

"A'ight, Don-Don. Wassup? If you called me I know it's important."

"I have a gift for you. Taste this." He pulled out a gram of pure cocaine wrapped in tin foil.

Kendu's mouth salivated with the idea of it as he pulled the strip of foil towards him. He took a quick snort, and it was so pure it felt like his brain was sprinkled with stardust. His dilated eyes opened wide, and he took his pinky and placed it in his mouth to savor every little bit. "Whoa! This shit is fire!" He cleared his throat, snorted and scratched his nose like a person with severe allergies. But it wasn't hay fever; it was coke fever. "That shit's pure as fuck! Damn! So, wassup? I need some of that. We're starving out there. My crew ain't had shit for over a month now."

"Starving, huh?" replied Don-Don with a very bland sympathetic look on his face. "Tell you what. I have a proposition for you." He leaned forward and folded his hands on top of his desk as though he was sharing some ancient secret. In almost a whisper-like tone he asked, "How long have you known me?"

"We been doing business for like over fifteen years."

"Yes, and haven't I always had your best interest in mind? How close are you and Supreme?"

"That's my nigga. Why? Wassup?"

"I'll give you two bricks to help me get rid of him."

Kendu's facial expression changed as rage raced through his bloodstream.

"Well, have I made you uncomfortable? That wasn't my intention. Before you jump to conclusions, let me make things clear. Me and my comrades are prepared for war. We can make what happened the other night an everyday thing. We have the money, and we have the expendable soldiers. But that can all be avoided. Look at it as a sacrifice. You give us Supreme, and we save a bunch of lives."

Don-Don was a cunning and persuasive older Haitian man with a talent for diplomacy and negotiation. However, his penchant for peace should have never be confused with anything but another sinister weapon in his arsenal. For him, diplomacy was a means to an end, not an end to his means.

Kendu was an opportunist, and his loyalty to Supreme consisted of two things; circumstantial and financial. "What you got against him anyway? Why the fuck do you want his head so bad?" he asked Don-Don.

"He has a dirty past that he cannot escape. He's betrayed people's trust and murdered loved ones. That is all the information I'm willing to give you. Now, make a decision. War or sacrifice. Walk out of here with some top of the line cocaine, or leave with a death wish, meaning this could be the last time we ever see one another." Don-Don's big piercing eyes looked directly into Kendu's spirit. His face expressed a sinful grin.

Kendu responded by abruptly cocking his Glock 9-mm

handgun. In a menacing manner he chambered a bullet and pointed it at Don-Don.

Don-Don's grin changed but his eyes did not move as he slowly leaned back in his office chair. Where another individual might have cowered in fear, he seemed to be amused by Kendu's threat. Don-Don folded his hands on the desk in front of him again and focused his attention on the barrel of the gun pointed at him. "So, what's that supposed to do? Like I said, make a decision." He then placed a bag containing four kilos of raw cocaine on the desk. "Now, here's some extra. Now! Choose!"

Kendu thought long and hard. His mind processed the fact that he was staring at over $100,000 worth of product wholesale, and even triple that if broken down and sold at retail. He snatched the bag off the desk and tucked his gun way before walking out, consumed by greed and guilt. He slammed the door behind him as he left.

After some moments passed, Don-Don called out, "You can come out now."

Bulla came out of the closet in Don-Don's office with a Mac-11 machinegun equipped with a silencer. "That was a good move, brethren. Now we save bullets *and* money. Me like how you move, mon," he said.

Don-Don smiled. "I told you that you didn't need that big ass gun."

"But you do owe me four kilos."

CHAPTER 26

THE TWIN TOWERS

"...I've been so paranoid,
I hear these niggas tryna fuck with me.
Real shit, I know I got enemies.
I can't let these niggas get to me.
I ain't scared to die.
Nigga, I'll take your life, nigga..."

"**P**ARANOID" by French Montana blared out of the sound system of Supreme's brand new 2013 BMW 50Si series. It was all black and tinted out, with a black leather interior, LED angel eye headlights, and black on chrome Lexani Wraith 22" rims.

Supreme hugged each corner as he swerved through Brooklyn traffic. He drove extra aggressively, as though his car was an extension of himself. He had woken up early to go pick up Freedom.

In the good old days it wouldn't have bothered Freedom having Supreme pick him up from the place where he slept. However, it was a new day and time. In Freedoms absence, the once great monument of brotherhood that they had built on a foundation of loyalty had withered. It was dilapidated and resembled ancient ruins.

Freedom paced back and forth on the corner of Fulton and Nostrand Avenue in Brooklyn, in front of the pizza shop.

"Ayo, Free!" bellowed Supreme as he turned the corner.

Freedom quickly opened the car door and sat down. He was smacked head-on by the aroma of sour diesel marijuana. "Damn, son! What the fuck is that? Shit smells strong. I smelled it as soon as you pulled up!"

"This's that loud, God, that all the young boys is fucking with. Here. You want to hit this?" Supreme said, and gestured to pass him the weed wrapped in Fronto leaves.

But Freedom refused. "You got any Percocets? My shoulder is aching," he asked.

Supreme reached in his pocket and pulled out a small Ziploc bag with about twenty 5-miligram Oxycotin pills.

"Good lookin' out, but I don't need all these shits. I don't fuck with them like that."

"Man, just keep 'em. Why you acting funny anyway?" Supreme then asked.

"Fuck you mean? Because I don't want to smoke right now? You on some hot boy shit anyway!"

The tension quickly escalated from zero to sixty mph.

"Are you serious, God? I held you down all them years. You was supposed to come home and get back in the game," Supreme responded.

He sped down Atlantic Avenue on his way to South Conduit. It was as if his temper accelerated with his vehicle. The faster he drove, the louder he spoke. "Nah, God, you acting funny. You changed. How the fuck you come home all incognito and shit? You think I ain't know you've been home? That shit is public record, God!"

"I had to gather my thoughts, my nigga. I just couldn't jump right back into it like that."

"I get it, God. You ain't built for this no more, that's all."

"Oh, 'cause I don't want to sniff coke and pop E-pills I ain't built for that life?"

Supreme put on a sinister smile. "Oh word? That's how you feel? You know we ain't kids no more."

"Jamaal, I get high, nigga! I don't give a fuck! I'm on my way out, man! Shit!" Freedom no longer cared to engage in this argument, and was utterly enraged to the point that the only thing that rivaled his anger was disgust for the individual that Supreme had become. "Pull over! I'm getting out!"

"No!"

"Nigga, you trying me, and I'm out before I do something I don't want to do!"

The car came to a screeching halt on Merrick Boulevard near Roy Wilkins Park. "So, get out!" Supreme yelled.

Freedom got out of the car. "Whatever, nigga!"

Supreme put the car in park and jumped out to continue antagonizing his once upon a time best friend.

A temperamental and highly volatile mixture of frustration, love and paranoia divided these two longtime comrades… or was it evolution and they had simply evolved in two separate directions?

"Supreme, stop pushing me, God!"

"Why? What you gonna do, killer? Huh? You 'bout that life." Now Supreme was completely in Freedom's face and blocking his path. He wasn't trying to belittle Freedom; it was just that his type of love came with aggression. It was a cry for help because the street life had gotten to him, and he needed to over saturate his body with drug after drug just to take his mind off the years of murder and betrayal.

Freedom represented a simpler time in his life when things were more peaceful. This was his brother, and in a sense it hurt him to feel like he was losing the one person that he could trust. In his sick, drug induced hypersensitive nature, he lashed out. "I knew I couldn't trust you! You probably had us setup that night!"

Something about the word "trust" really got to Freedom. "Trust? You mean like trust my brother not to fuck my bitch?"

Somewhat taken aback by the extent of Freedom's knowledge, Supreme still responded in his own defense. "That's why you acting emotional like a bitch over a dead whore!"

In that instant, Freedom slugged Supreme in the face with a solid but sloppy right hook. The punch wasn't thrown with the cold, calculated accuracy of an opponent. It was more like the fury of an angry sibling who was fighting because of his emotions.

The punch sent both men to the ground with Supreme landing underneath Freedom. They wrestled on the ground for some time like two male lions competing for the alpha role within the pride. With Freedom getting the best of the conflict, he got up off of Supreme and rose to his feet expecting a striking match.

All the rules of engagement had been thrown out of the window. Supreme barely got to his feet before he charged at his friend like a defensive linebacker, digging his shoulder into Freedom's gut and slamming him back to the ground and scuffing up is brand new Timberland construction boots.

Freedom took the advantage by wrapping his arms around his opponent's neck and putting him in a frontal headlock.

"You gonna chill now?" he yelled through his bloody lips.

But Supreme wasn't so easily subdued. The more he struggled, the more Freedom put his weight on Supreme's neck. Supreme wiggled his way out of the headlock and both men scrambled to their feet,

Before Freedom could gather his bearings and mount another assault, he was staring down the barrel of a nickel-plated .45 caliber Desert Eagle. He shortened the distance between him and the gun and pressed his forehead firmly against the muzzle. "You got the drop now, God. Good move, nigga. Now, what you gonna do?" he asked. His thoughts were moving at the speed of light, yet everything slowed down to a complete standstill. This wasn't his first time staring at the wrong end of a gun, but it could definitely be his last. "If you gonna shoot, then shoot!"

Supreme and Freedom locked eyes and mirrored one another's souls, each searching for their childhood friend; looking for innocence and digging for a moment of solace. Neither one could find any good in the other. They were far removed from their childhood dreams and times of mischievous adventures. Now they were each looking at a stone cold murderer. They were like apex predators circling one another and anticipating their foe's next move.

Freedom was close enough to grab the gun, but he didn't want to make any sudden moves.

Supreme's eyes had bags under them. He was stressed and overmedicated with drugs. He had painted himself into a corner by unintentionally drawing his weapon out of sheer instinct. And now he was faced with the most difficult decision of his life: "*Should I kill the only person I trust? Is the principal that important?*" His arm trembled and his eyes welled up with tears. The gun shook in his hand until he brought his arm down. "I love you, God!" he said as he embraced his brother.

Freedom reluctantly uttered, "I love you too," while rolling his eyes behind Supreme's back.

In that instant, despite the fact that neither was murdered, their union had just been destroyed before their eyes.

Coming to their senses and seeing the onlookers in the distance who had stopped and pulled out their phones in an attempt to record the conflict, they jumped back into the car and sped off.

"Yo, why the fuck was everybody pointing their phones at us?" Freedom asked.

"I forgot you been gone for a while. This is the new 'social media' age. You got to be careful because everybody's got cameras in their phones, and niggas record everything and put it on line."

"You serious? It sounds like niggas is snitching on themselves now."

A short period of time had passed and an awkward silence filled the air. There wasn't much left to be said or done. Silently, they mourned the death of their friendship. Both men were disheveled from their endeavors, and mentally there was a roadblock for them to get through before they could ever be the same. In any other climate these two would have parted ways as mortal enemies.

But a storm was approaching, and Lady Death's shadow was slowly creeping. The demons from their past were steadily approaching. So, even though their comradery was steadily diminishing, they would be forced to unite under the commonality of war.

"So, why did you come get me and bring me all the way out here?" Freedom asked.

"'Cause we need to figure out how we're going to handle this shit wit' those fucking monkeys."

"Oh, okay. We could have did that in Brooklyn."

"I wanted to get you some clothes too, God. You can't be running around looking like 1999 out here, nigga."

"Well, I ain't wearing all that super tight shit these little niggas is wearing either,"

They shared a quick smile, and it was back to business.

"Those motherfuckers is Jamaicans, God. Fucking Fire must got family all over this motherfucker," Supreme said.

"Yeah. I had two hits on my head from Sopa and Bulla."

"I know, son. This shit's got to end."

"Once and for all. You know when I was locked up I used to go over shit in my head, like how long are we gonna keep killing each other... like when will it stop?" Freedom then put his head down as tears started to flow. "They killed Samaya, man, Why her? Why Samaya?"

"I don't know, my nigga. I don't know. But we going to end this shit right now!"

Freedom continued to have an emotional breakdown. He had been holding it together for so long, and it was as though all his thoughts were collapsing down on him at once. "I saw pictures of her. You can't imagine what they did to her, and they did it to get back at me. They chopped her up, man!" With bloodshot eyes and tears streaming down his face, he had a look of pure bloodlust. "I'm going to kill Sopa, but I'm going to take my time with him! I'ma torture that motherfucker!"

"You need me in on that, I'm wit' you."

"Nah, I got a plan for him. He's not even gonna see me coming.

What I need is for you to find Bulla and Magnum and blow their fucking heads off."

"Now that's the Freedom I know! Consider it done! And what about the business?" Supreme asked.

"I got connects that're in the Feds. Let's clear this beef and then get back to business. But listen to me, God. One more flip, and I'm out. I can't keep doing this shit. I got a daughter to live for."

"I feel the same way, man. I'm just tired... tired of all the bullshit that comes with this shit."

CHAPTER 27

EL DIABLO

HECTOR was a rising star in the illustrious but deadly business of pushing illegal pharmaceuticals. He stayed on Dyckman, a neighborhood well known for being one of the east coast's cocaine capitols.

However, that is not the only thing that Washington Heights is known for. It's also the home of one of the largest and most sophisticated medical facilities; Columbia Presbyterian Hospital. But even more importantly, Washington Heights, over the past four decades, has become a home away from home for many Dominicans. It was a hub for a robust stew of Dominican food and culture.

Hector a.k.a. Diablo was able to thrive in his native community. Coming from humble beginnings, he was the meaning of "The American Dream". His story was the same as many immigrants from his homeland, save for the fact that he chose the illegal route, while most chose to be law abiding citizens and take whatever work they could get. Many even opened their own businesses in the community and were pushing the American economy farther through entrepreneurship.

Diablo earned his name as a sinister cutthroat hitman who killed his own father for a position in the hierarchy of *Sangre de Jesus*.

On this particular day he sat in the living room of one of his apartments on Post Avenue. This was his stronghold. He sold a lot of weight from that building. It was five stories high with one entrance and exit, and was located in an excellent place that was connected to many major highways making it easy to get to for out of towners.

Diablo controlled the building. It was his fortress, with different aspects of his business on each floor. He had an apartment for processing and stretching cocaine; another for converting soft to hard; and an apartment for packaging. He never kept money on the premises, but there was security everywhere. Each floor had a checkpoint. What could casually appear to be young kids hanging around joking on each floor were actually lookouts and armed foot soldiers.

Diablo sat in his chair watching the hit TV show, "The Wire" while blasting Style-P:

> *"...Monopolizing on how this game is being played,*
> *Every day I think about if she would of stayed.*
> *Anyway, this paper be calling.*
> *This is not a dream,*
> *I write rhymes to keep from falling.*
> *Try not to sleep..."*

Long pulls of purple Kush created clouds in the air that filled the apartment with a marijuana mist. The three bedroom apartment on the fifth floor was rattling from the speakers. It was amazing that Diablo heard the doorbell.

A beautiful young woman went over to the door and looked out the peephole. "Hector, it's somebody from Time Warner Cable. Let him in?" she asked.

"Bitch, I told you not to say my fucking government name! Yeah, let the muthafucka in!"

Paula opened the door. A short, young man with glasses and clean shaven walked in, intent on getting his job done.

Diablo said, "So, you came to fix this shit, right? Some maintenance shit? Well hurry the fuck up!" He was an obnoxious bastard who enjoyed intimidating people, and Pistola will enjoy killing him.

Pistola spun around revealing a sharp screwdriver from his tool bag. He gave Diablo the embrace of death. The first thrust was low and close to his waistline, puncturing his external oblique muscle. The thrust second hit a kidney. They were rapid and short. Pistola quickly placed his hand over Diablo's mouth and guided his body back to the couch, stabbing him ten times in total.

He then tapped a button on the hollowed out cable box to reveal a Glock-9 equipped with a silencer and extended cartridge. It was getting messy, and it was supposed to be neat and quiet.

Diablo had a lot of security. The original plan was to take the gun out at the door and come in blazing, taking them with the element of surprise. But the two soldiers in the hallway gave him a need to innovate. They say that necessity is the mother of invention, so the screwdriver came in handy.

Unfortunately, Paula had to take one in the head as she came rushing into the room, splitting her forehead. Her body went limp and she fell to the floor.

Pistola stood over Diablo as he lay there dying and squirming on his back and choking on his own blood. Pistola felt merciful and put one slug between his eyes. After all, Diablo was his brother—not by blood, but ethnicity.

No one really loves that life. Most are just trying to feed their families. Some, however—a rare few—a unique breed—are chosen for the streets. These same individuals would make excellent businessmen. Pistola was a professional hitman, not by choice but bred that way.

He checked every room in the apartment, gun first and ready to give anyone a head shot.

The music was loud. The foot soldiers in the hallway couldn't have heard anything between the music and their loud smoke-filled bravado.

Pistola placed the gun back in its hidden compartment in the cable box and quickly exited the apartment, closing the door behind him. The young hoods in the hallway didn't even consider him a threat.

As he started down the steps one of the young teens lightly slapped the back of his head and kicked him in the butt.

Pistola pulled his hat down and grinned. "Stop, man! I didn't do nothing!" And he continued to walk down the stairs faster, grinning all the way out the front door. He was pleased with the accuracy of his costume, and it was just more feasible to leave quietly and avoid a shootout.

CHAPTER 28

PURPLE RAIN

THE singers; the greats that represented the sound of Black culture; the legends, the demigods who laid the foundation and standards for greatness, have ascended to the heavens. The Michael Jackson's and the Whitney Houston's have all died leaving us holding onto our contemporary figures—not in a sense of being fans, but having an ancestral voice; someone to tell you how it is, and like it was through song.

Now? Well, all the young have is gadgets: computers, YouTube, social media whose popularity grew exponentially from Myspace, which was a phenomenon, only to be crushed by Facebook, which spawned a number of others like Instagram, etc.

******

Sixteen year old Rain sat comfortably in her room which was a little cramped, but it was safe. She watched "Game of Thrones" while talking on her iPhone and doing her homework on her laptop.

She kept her hair natural. It was a perfect mixture. It was soft but not too soft as her mother's was, and jet black and curly like her fathers. Her skin was reddish-brown, and her eyes were slightly slanted like her mother's. She just recently got to the point where getting her hair and nails done was weekly maintenance. She was the best part of Freedom and Samaya.

Rain tried not to rebel against her grandmother too much, but like a lot of teenagers at that time, she liked to wear tight True Religion jeans, but remained as classy as possible. She also loved rappers like J. Cole and Kendrick Lamar.

"Knock! Knock! Knock!"

"Who is it? Damn! Y'all chicks got to wait. I ain't braiding nobody's hair until I finish my homework!" Rain shouted. She was pushing to get into Columbia University's honorary program. While attending Bronx Science High School may have been prestigious, an early scholarship to Columbia would be exceptional. She never cracked under pressure, and always rose to the challenge.

"Knock! Knock! Knock!"

"Who?" she shouted.

"It's your father."

"Oh, you mean 'Jamaal'? Come in," she said sarcastically before she quickly jumped up, unlocked her door and got right back to her work.

"Excuse me, young lady. What did you just say?"

"I said 'Jamaal'."

"Is that how you feel?"

"Is that how I feel? *Is that how I feel?*" she repeated, her voice escalating while her eyes filled with tears. "I've waited for you for fifteen years, and you were never around! Don't come into my life way after the fact and try to play daddy!"

Freedom was torn, but he was humble—not in the negative sense, but in the sense that he was faced with humility. This little woman stood up to him. She faced him and mirrored rage. She was a product of his love and his hate.

"And just when I would have reconsidered and said okay, my Dad is an O.G. I could have respected that, and when he came home he was going to change his life! But no! You get my mother killed over your bullshit!"

Freedom moved toward her. He was annoyed by her words, but he held himself back and gestured "Shh!" with his index finger over his lips, and gently but firmly grabbed her arm.

"What're you gonna do? Hit me? Beat me? Huh? That's the only way you know how to fix things, right? Get off my arm!" she pulled her arm away from his grip.

"That's how you really feel? There are things I had no power over, honey."

"Do you even know who killed her?" Rain asked.

"No."

"No? Well I do!" She quickly got on her laptop, minimized her homework and opened up four other screens. She pulled up a picture of Sopa from the Federal Most Wanted list. "His real name is Emilio Delgado."

Apparently Rain was a whiz kid, and upon the death of her mother, she switched her focus. At first she was more into computer programing for the sake of building video game constructs.

But that morphed into a passion self-educating herself on criminal justice and UNIX/Linux, which are software used on government mainframes and super computers.

"Okay, so you're a hacker."

"No, Jamaal, I'm not a hacker. I just know how to tap into certain satellite surveillance. I'm sure that Sopa ordered the hit, and the murderer had to be someone else." Rain was not stoic at all. She put all her rage, frustration and emotions into finding her mother's killer.

Freedom was shocked by his daughter's extensive knowledge and knowhow. However, as proud and impressed as he was, there was also a touch of fear because her knowledge made her dangerous. "How many people know that you have access to this information?" he asked.

"Nobody. Jamaal, don't start playing Daddy now."

Freedom almost lost his temper. "Look, little girl! I know I wasn't always there for you. I have my reasons, and you're entitled to have your personal hostilities, because as a young woman you're dealing with a lot. But I don't give a fuck! You will not be calling me 'Jamaal' like I'm your fucking friend! If you can't call me 'Dad', then don't call me anything at all!"

Rain's eyes welled up with tears and her extra rough exterior melted away. She had spent the last couple of months building a wall around her emotions and burying herself in her academic pursuits; anything to keep her mind off of the murder of her mother and step-father. In that moment the butterflies in her stomach fluttered. Her upper lip trembled and she balled out in utter agony of a poor defenseless child missing the warmth and security that only a mother's breast can provide.

So, as she cried out and clung to her father for strength, she made one request that seemed to spill from her lips mixed with saliva and tears. "Daddy, please don't leave me again! I can't take losing you too! Can I ask you a question?"

"Yes."

"Is it possible to hate and love someone at the same time?"

"Yes, it is possible, honey. Trust me; I hate myself for what happened to your mother."

They sat in silence for a moment, as though their hearts spoke without words.

Freedom pitied her because he knew what it was like to feel abandoned. He knew the posttraumatic stress caused by a traumatizing childhood, and all he could do was rock her back and forth in his arms. And for once in over a decade, they were father and daughter again.

CHAPTER 29

DIABLO LIVES

PISTOLA was bred and raised to be the most deadly and calculated murderer. Killing Diablo was easier than he expected. The only dangerous part was picking up his payment afterwards.

As he was driving, he got an anonymous call on his cell phone. *"Hola!* Who is this?" he asked.

"You know who this is. Meet me at 1526 St. Nicholas Ave., Apartment 42."

It was a familiar voice on the other end of the line, so the phone call meant one of three things: Either he was going to collect a major payday; make an important business connection, or someone was trying to set him up. One thing was for certain; Pistola was well-prepared for whatever may come his way. He was carrying a fully loaded Glock-19 equipped an with ECO-9 silencer so he could slay in silence.

Every move Pistola made was premeditated. Remorse and sympathy were two luxuries that he could not afford. He buried his humanity deep below his narrow beady eyes and slight features. His low Caesar style haircut was only unique because of the sharp contrast between his jet black, coarse straight hair and beige complexion. He was a chameleon, able to blend in with any group.

Although he didn't like his profession, he stuck to it because being solo for so many years had taught him one thing: he's actually good at it.

******

Everyone has a secret love for "the killers" in society. There is something that the media overall glorifies about that individual who has enough fortitude to calmly take another life. As much as society contradicts itself every chance it gets by persecuting and demonizing the same thing, it praises in television and music. We get these repeated messages saying "Stand up for yourself; just don't stand up against us! Speak for yourself; just don't speak up against us!" Somehow the masses have fallen victim to this indoctrination of helplessness.

But in the midst of all these zombies, you have the anomalies; the enigmas like Pistola, and like Freedom. People who make their own rules love it or hate it, but you must respect it.

******

Pistola had switched out of his Time Warner Cable uniform and was jogging up the steps of 1526 St. Nicholas Ave., looking for Apartment 42. He was anxious to get there and receive his pay. He was extremely apprehensive while jogging up the four flights of stairs in his gray Nike sweat suit and Airforce Ones to match. The adrenaline was still racing from the previous kill.

Pistola was armed and ready for any mishap that might take place while collecting his fee from this anonymous benefactor. It was a risky business being a gun for hire. The road was filled with mishaps and uncertainties while you, the killer, must remain certain, disciplined and imaginative.

"Knock! Knock! Knock!"

He was greeted by a familiar voice that said, "Come inside, Pistolito!"

As he pushed open the door and walked down the corridor, he could hear a group of Dominican men speaking in Spanish. But their words and cadence were as unique as the island they hailed from.

There was something familiar about this setup. That voice that called his name, it was something from his past.

Pistola was greeted by a group of well-dressed older men. Their scowls were in no way welcoming, but he was not there to make friends. Everyone stood their frozen, like it was a Mexican standoff. Pistola was silent. His eyes were locked on the crowd of men.

Slowly, everyone in the room began to move accordingly. There were no sudden movements. Everything was gradual. Hands reached for weapons and the tension in the room was so thick that you could hardly breathe.

Pistola was clearly outgunned, but pride would not allow him to retreat. His natural reflexes kicked in as he grabbed the rubber gripped handle of his gun.

Before that tiny apartment in Washington Heights became a complete warzone, Sopa emerged from behind the crowd like a ghost, and Pistola froze—not from fear, but from shock. For years he had despised Sopa and swore to kill him. But as much as he loathed him, he also loved him. Standing before him was the only father he ever knew.

"You look good, Pistola. And I see you've grown well."

It was a sinister reunion of master and mad scientist. Sopa wasn't sure whether he could trust Pistola despite his gut feelings. This was his son; maybe not through blood, but through bloodshed. Sopa had taught him everything and bred him to be a complete killing machine void of morality.

Pistola had evolved into his own man; confident and resilient. He was no longer the little boy that Sopa remembered.

"What's wrong, *hijo?* You look like you seen a ghost. Aren't you happy to see me?" Sopa's cynical tone only added to an already precarious situation.

"Of course I'm glad to see you, Papa. I just thought you were dead." Pistola's quick witted answer might have saved his life, and he knew it.

Sopa turned to his comrades, Flako, Gato and Joselito and gestured for them to relax. Gato put his butterfly knife away with a look of disappointment on his face.

"So, why go through all this? Why not just contact me? Why send me on a job anonymously?" Pistola asked.

"I had to test you first, *hijo.* I had to know that you were the same Pistola that I made. Plus, I just wanted to observe your work. It was cute. A little sloppy, but I give you credit for being able to improvise, because I didn't know how you would be able to get past Diablo's security. A cable guy! Nice! Very professional. Have you seen Freedom?"

"No. Ain't he in the Feds?"

"He's been home for damn near a year. Why haven't you been doing intel on our enemies? Or is he not our enemy?" Sopa asked and took a long hard stare into Pistola's eyes. He was searching for a sign, but he couldn't find one.

Sopa needed a face; someone to represent him in the streets of New York. His fugitive status forced him to play the shadows. Despite having some of the best assassins that S.D.J. (Sangre de Jesus) had to offer, he still needed people who knew the terrain. Sopa needed Pistola. "Listen to me. I need you to do something for me."

"How much?"

"How much you want?"

"Depends."

"On what?"

"On who you want dead."

"I don't want anybody dead. I want them alive and brought here to kneel in front of me."

"Who do you want to kneel?"

"Freedom. I want that fucking Moreno in front of me on his knees. That piece of shit cost me millions of dollars and damn near killed my family. I've got a tight squeeze on him now. I hit the fucker where it hurts; took his love away. So at least if we can't find him, he'll have to find us."

"I can take care of that, Papa. Trust me."

Sopa gestured to Joselito, who stepped forward with a book bag full of cash. "That should cover the work you just did, and I put a little extra as a down payment for your next project."

"Papa, I'm your eyes to see, you ears to hear, and I'm your hands to reach out and touch."

"*Hijo*, it is our time now. We've spent years preparing for this. There are millions to be made in this city. I've got all the warriors I need," Sopa said, pointing to Gato and Flaco. "Now, I need someone to lead my soldiers and teach them how to maneuver in this city."

At that moment Pistola's phone rang.

"Who's that?" Sopa asked him.

"Business. I got another meeting. I got to go," Pistola replied. Apparently it was Freedom calling his phone.

Sopa spoke suspiciously. "So, you're not going to hang around for a while? Don't you miss me? Hang out for a while. Sip a little Brugal."

"Right after I handle some business," Pistola said, and flung the book bag full of over $30,000 over his shoulder. The wheels in his mind were turning at light speed. He rushed out of the building to answer his phone, but in the midst of his uncertainty he chose to ignore Freedom's call.

Pistola was engaged in a hazardous game filled with trickery and deception. The only advantage he had over Sopa was the fact that he was needed.

The one thing about Sopa was that he discarded anything he felt wasn't useful.

Now, Freedom was honestly Pistola's true ally. But if faced with the same dilemma, would he stay loyal?

Life in a nutshell was a proverbial chess game where the winner takes all. This war consisted of many battles. It is a lifetime of moments. Each of these battles or moments collectively make up our lives.

Pistola paused for a moment at the edge of the crossroads. On one hand, Freedom had earned his trust and loyalty. On the other hand, there was Sopa, who proved to be very disloyal and sinister.

However, what Sopa lacked in comradery, he compensated for with money and flamboyant charisma.

Pistola was resolute in his decision. He had to do what was best. Really and truly, it wasn't about Freedom *or* Sopa. It was about him; his life, his death, his honor as a man. He made his choice, and he had exited the room with a dark and chilling prediction. "Give me a few days. I'll bring him to you."

CHAPTER 30

CROCODILE DEM WORK

WARRIOR drove his red van down Nostrand Avenue, weaving through traffic. He pulled over in front of the many buildings he was a superintendent for. The van reeked of gas, among other things.

He parked, jumped out, opened the basement door and quickly unloaded all of his supplies onto a flatbed hand truck. There was plaster, sheetrock, and one particularly heavy garbage bag.

It was a beautiful day in Brooklyn, and children were playing outside. "Excuse me, Mr. Your bag is leaking," one of them said.

Warrior quickly dragged his things inside and returned to spray the entry walkway with bleach.

Once inside the basement, he began to unload his tools consisting of hammers, saws, rubber gloves and an apron. He turned on what he called "work music":

"...*Rifle wave, slap five in ya ears,*
Man a dive in a grave,
Ya a try fi be brave.
From box truck and marble,
And bicycle days,
Man step wid the gun,

Mothers frightened fi days…"
          "Crocodile Dem Work" by dancehall artist, Masika.

Warrior stood 6'2" and weighed 240 pounds. He looked like a black power lifter in his ripped jeans and fitted white shirt. The residents of his buildings knew him as Mr. Benjamin. But in the streets of Brooklyn all the way back to the streets of Tivoli Gardens, Jamaica, he was known as "Warrior", a heartless killer—or at least that's how the legend goes.

In America he took the short road to success while others hustled hard to push narcotics. He focused on being the "muscle". He was an enforcer for hire. His loyalty belonged to the highest bidder. He was a one stop shot for hits and waste disposal, if you know what I mean.

Before he could open up the garbage bag and get to work, the doorbell rang. *"It must be one of the annoying tenants,"* he thought. "A, wha di bumbaclot who a go ring me bell when me just reach?"

A recognizable voice called from the other side of the door, "Open de door, cousin! Wha happen? Yuh paranoid?"

Warrior opened the door for his cousins, Magnum and Bulla. Magnum was his usual self; dapper as ever dressed in a G-Star Raw denim suit, while Bulla remained a Rasta to the bone, with a pair of Lucky Brand jeans and a Bob Marley shirt. Bulla stayed basic and camouflaged as possible.

"So, wha make me family come a foreign. Me know yuh nah come fi check me."

"No, mon. We find di man who a kill Fire!" said Magnum.

"For real?"

"Yeah. I wan give dem bwoy some real shot inna dem blood clot!"

"Can me jus finish a work while we chat?" Warrior asked, and lay down a large piece of plastic tarp. Then he dragged a limp dead body out of the very large industrial strength garbage bag.

Much to Bulla and Magnum's discomfort, Warrior began by breaking each one of the corpse's fingers, then each toe. He had an assortment of saws and blades that were able to break bones and cut flesh. "First t'ing ya wan do when ya break down de body, ya afi make small pieces so when ya t'row de body inna acid or de fire, it burn up quick, ya see me?" he explained.

Magnum began to speak in between the ever present sound of bones snapping while ligaments and flesh tore. "Yeah, mon. So we need a lickle assistance for de t'ing. We have a nice setup and we a work wit' a next mon, Don-Don."

"A who ya mean? Haitian Don-Don in Queens?"

"Yeah. Me done some work wit' dat bwoy dere."

Bulla interrupted and spoke in a firm yet soft voice. "Listen. Point is, we don trust one a dem bwoys, so when de money exchange, everybody ago dead. Only we t'ree ago walk out, understand? Me Nah care 'bout no one, understand? Man a kill Fire, and over ten bombaclot years ago pass and mon a still walk. No, mon. Supreme, Freedom, Don-Don and whoever afi dead!"

"Me hear yuh, lickle brudda. Me hear. You don't worry ya self, mon. Me gwan handle it. Trust me."

"Yo, Bulla, why Don-Don? Him afi help we. Why gwan kill him?" Magnum asked.

Bulla sucked his teeth and snarled before turning his head slowly towards Magnum, forcing one of his long, clumpy old locks to cover his eye. This added to his already piercing glare and angry scowl. "Because, we gwam kill off the whole a dem blood clots and take over de whole fucking t'ing. You a gwan like revenge alone, me need! Nah, mon. Dogs afi eat food, hear me, bredren?"

Warrior gave his favorite cousins a reassuring nod while snapping an elbow.

Magnum respected his big brother's terms, but he was also at a lack for words because the scent of the corpse was turning his stomach. "Yo, family. Me gwan link you lickle more seen." He moved to give Warrior a fist bump but quickly reversed that decision when he noticed the grotesque chunks of flesh all over his rubber gloves. He rushed out, covering his mouth because of nausea.

"Bulla, ya lickle brudda still soft. Wha happen to him?" Warrior asked.

Bulla gave a slight grin, which he never does, but seeing his older cousin was like seeing an old friend. No one except Rita knew Bulla like Warrior did. "Him nah grow rough like we. Plus, for truth, him strong wit' him machine, but him nah real gunmon. Him a hustle, understand?"

"Ya, mon. You need dat for real. Can't have murder and no money. But listen here. Ya see me. Dis a small t'ing fa me. Me jus afi eliminate evidence. Yah see me and me do a lickle work for big money. But you, bredren, you is smart. Me never wan dis life fo yah. Sometimes me look 'pon your life an blame myself."

"Hold on! Hold on! Hold on! Nah, mon! Ya can't do dat, boss.

Ya can't t'ink a big fifty bombaclot five year old mon like me self want sympathy or well wishes, blessings and prayers. But ya see, I is a man who na chop up or burn up a body. Nah, mon. Me kill mon right where him stand. Me no care 'bout police or revenge or anyt'ing. So trust me, big cousin Warrior. Me and me alone take blame for wha me do! Anyway, still back to work, mon. Me gwan."

"Yes, lickle brudda. Lock de door. Bless!"

CHAPTER 31

ZARABANDA

THE *djembe* drums were vibrating the air as seven older men in their early sixties pounded them with their palms. The synchronicity was beautiful. They all seemed to be in tune.

The *djembe* is an African percussion instrument classified as a membranophone. It is mostly made of a hollowed out wooden cylinder topped off with stretched animal hide. It is the primary instrument of choice in many African centered religious ceremonies.

The traditional rhythms hypnotized Freedom. He had never been anywhere so rich in African culture. There was an energy coursing through the room, and he couldn't quite put his finger on it.

Nefertarie had convinced Freedom to go with her to visit her godmother, Ifa Abeyo, and her godfather, who both happen to be high ranking priests or *paleros* in the Palo Mayombe Spiritual School of Thought. Palo, or La Reglas de Congo, is a spiritual system that finds its roots in the Congo of Africa. But it was cultivated in Cuba by Central African slaves.

On this particular day it was a celebration for the children of Zarabanda, a fierce spirit known to be a strong protector. He is the head over weapons of bloodshed, like knives and blades, so healing and arming are both of his to control. He is considered the god of war, and is known for being raw, and possessing unquenchable energy.

They were deep in Brooklyn on the borderline of Brownsville and East New York, inside a shabby old house on 638 Warwick Street, right around the corner from the Number 3 Train at its final stop on New Lots Avenue. The entire first floor of the house was decorated in the colors preferred by the spirit, which for Zarabanda were green, black and red or coral, all paired off into sets of seven. Seven green candles stood in a row, and seven green curtains covered the windows.

Freedom could easily point out the initiates from the neophytes. The initiates, like Nefertarie, wore all white and had a green or coral sash across their chests. Many of the initiates walked around singing ritual songs.

As the drums intensified, Freedom could feel his heart pounding as though it was one with the beat. He couldn't quite figure out what he was doing in this place. The last thing he expected was a full-fledged Voodoo ceremony happening right in front of him. He just knew that he followed Nefertarie. He was nervous and his palms were sweating. The Afro-Latin beat seemed to vibrate his soul while the rhythmic chanting of the initiates heightened the hypnotic effect. Where anyone else might have been spooked out by the activities, Freedom seemed to find something harmonious about it all.

Some of the initiates had cigars in their mouths that were turned around backwards. They were blowing smoke all over and into iron pots. Each pot was decorated differently, but were very similar.

At that point Nefertarie happened to walk over to him. "Babe, what are those?" he asked her.

"Those are *las prendas*, or altars."

He then pointed at some very weird looking statues and asked, "And those?"

"Those are Nkisi's. Both of those and *la prenda* are considered doorways to the spirit realm."

"So why are they blowing smoke on them and spitting out rum? And shit! What the fuck is all this?"

"This, Free, is how the spirits are fed, and then you ask your favor."

"So, if these spirits are so strong, why do they need people to feed them?"

"Silly ass! It's deeper than just that. Anyway, come and follow me. Meet my godmother. Her name is Ifa Abeyo. She's the highest ranking *palera* in my family."

"Okay, I'll meet with her real quick. Then I have to go. You know I got a lot of shit to take care of tonight."

"I know. That's exactly why you need to see my *palera*."

The energy was kinetic as Freedom moved through the crowd with the lovely Nefertarie holding his hand. Dressed all in white, to him she was nothing less than a ghetto angel. Her beautiful dark brown skin only seemed to add to her more than regal demeanor.

She quickly led him through the crowd of patrons, bringing him before Ifa Abeyo.

Ifa Abeyo was a thick, dark skinned woman with very slight features. Freedom held out his hand to greet her, but she gestured for him to sit down in front of her. She examined him quickly before handing him a piece of paper and a pen. "Okay, sweetheart. Write down your full name and date of birth," she instructed.

"Why? What for?"

Ifa looked at him with pity, and simply nodded her head. "Listen here, puddin'. You got things going on. You got too much going on. Okay, I don't need your name or birthday, 'cause I see Zarabanda all over you, child. I'm going to tell you something that I shouldn't. But since you came here with my daughter, and I know that she loves you, I'm going to give you the benefit of the doubt. This thing you're doing here, it's dangerous. I see a lot of danger around you."

Freedom gave Ifa direct eye contact, and in peering deep into her old eyes, it was as though he saw the universe. Her eyes seemed almost black. Her voice was an anomaly in of itself; a feminine baritone that soothed. She was dressed in ivory garments from head to toe, with her head completely wrapped in a crown made of white cloth. She had an uncanny ability to peek directly into his soul. For Freedom, this was an awkward moment, but it felt appropriate.

The false images that the media creates around African centered spirituality came crumbling down to dust. Freedom's eyes were opened. His senses had awakened, and Ifa's voice became the song, while the *djembe* his heartbeat.

Freedom's eyelids began to flutter, and visions ran through his mind like snippets of film. So many faces were recognizable and indescribable: Sopa, Nefertarie, Mercedes, Supreme, Fire, Pistola, Chyna, Reggie, Hashish, Samaya, Rain and Ifa.

"You have an army of ancestors who work through you. Your path is the path of your father. You will go through this war. He will clear the pathway for you. He will prepare you. Remember to only use your blade for a righteous cause. You are moving towards greatness, but you have been going through trials and tests. The redemption that you are looking for is right in front of you. Trust that. The spirit says that you will have to make a choice. You have been through the worst part already, but that choice, puddin', will forever alter your path."

Ifa then giggled before continuing. "As though it ain't been altered enough!"

Something about a spiritual reading is that there's an intimate moment between the spiritual practitioner and the client, patient or person being read. The person getting the reading has to open up and be vulnerable enough to let someone in, while the reader has to be insightful, respectful and unobtrusive. The end result is a somewhat mutual trance where two people are literally having the same supernatural experience.

Ifa's voice seemed to switch from and older Haitian lady from New York to a deep New Orleans Geechee drawl. "And puddin', you listen. That little girl; protect that little girl, you hear me? Your power colors are black, red and purple. You got the Baron with you at all times. Work with him. And connect with Zarabanda. That's enough for now. I could go on and on about you, puddin', with yo' fine self! You're okay, baby." She then gently placed her hand on his face.

Freedom's eyelids stopped fluttering. He was totally coherent and had heard every word.

"Nefertarie, where did you get this piece of chocolate?" Ifa asked.

"That's Uncle Mike's friend."

"Is he taken?"

"He most certainly is!"

"Shit, girl! I know that's right! I ain't mad at you."

CHAPTER 32

BLACK WIDOW

Dear 'Preme:

I love you, and I will always love you, but I can't continue on like this. Over the past years I've had three miscarriages.

You just can't stop cheating! It's bad enough that I worry about you running around all crazy in the streets. You keep saying you're going to change, but you never do. I know I fucked up with Cash, but that shit was ten years ago, and that's all you keep bringing up. At this point, that shit's just a motherfucking excuse. You don't love anybody but yourself.

I just realized there's something better out there, and I don't need this shit of you out there fucking other bitches. You know what, Basil? I fucking hate you! That's it! Fuck you! Good-bye! And don't try to find me. I'm getting an Order of Protection, so come near me, your ass is going back to jail!

Yes, I'm pregnant, and no, I'm not keeping it. Fuck you! Have a nice life. I hope you don't get shot dead in the street or go to jail and get raped in your ass, you fucking faggot! Good-bye forever!

Sincerely yours,
Chyna

******

SUPREME came home to an empty house. The furniture and three plasma screen HD TV's were gone. All Chyna left him was his bed, guns, some of his money, a pregnancy test and a good-bye letter. She had left hours ago and moved to a hidden location.

Sometimes you can break or woman or push her to the farthest extent to where she feels trapped and caged in, and she must get away. Chyna had to run. With the murder of her friend, together with Supreme's proclivity for violence and infidelity, she was at her wits end. And frankly, well into her 30's, she had grown up and no longer felt that being the wife of a drug lord was appealing. She wanted to be free of looking over her shoulder, and she wanted her child to have a better life.

The whole idea of even dealing with Supreme was that she saw his potential to evolve. But her expectations were never met, and the older he got, the more of a gangster he became, while she went to school to study law and worked part time as a paralegal. Being affiliated with him alone could easily destroy her aspirations to become a district attorney.

Supreme took his time reading the handwritten letter. Every word jumped off of the page. His long locks seemed to form a cage around the letter. He could hear Chyna's voice in his ear while he read. He could visualize her every expression. He could hear her voice and every subtle cadence.

He found a positive pregnancy test. He was hurt emotionally, but he foresaw their relationship coming to an end. Yet, there was nothing he could do to prevent it.

In that instant, his second greatest love left him because he couldn't leave his first love alone, and her name was "The Streets".

Supreme was married to the streets. He was addicted to the hustle. It still gave him a rush.

Supreme's heart was cold as he pulled a bottle of Hennessey from the cabinet and dropped two little pieces of Molly into it before commencing to gulp it down. The drug abuse was all part of the lifestyle. He needed something to distract his mind from the pain.

His eyes were dry. He just couldn't cry. He had seen too much to cry. He had done too much to regret.

He unfolded a brand new hundred dollar bill with a half a gram of coke in it. He raised it to his nose and snorted it until it was gone. He just needed some type of "pick-me-up".

Supreme was lonely. He felt like he lost Chyna, Freedom... even his entire family had turned their backs on him. All he was left with was Kendu and a plethora of others that he didn't trust.

To be alone in solitude is such a cruel self-defining space where the biggest adversities are your thoughts... *"Do your thoughts block you? Or do they unleash you? Do your thoughts keep you submerged in self-pity, regret and guilt? Or do they inspire, uplift and rejuvenate?"*

At that moment, Supreme was in a dark place. Someone had to die. He put the muzzle of his Glock into his mouth, took the gun off safety and closed his eyes, preparing to meet the Grim Reaper and finally be free from the shackles of humanity.

Then his phone rang and he took the gun out of his mouth as he had done many times before. "Yo, peace. Who dis?"

"Freedom."

"How you don't know my math? You don't ever call."

"What up wit' you?"

"Nothing. Chyna left me."

"Aww man, God! You alright? You good?"

"Yeah. Fuck that bitch!"

"Come on, God. You've been with her for like twenty years. You don't mean that."

"Man, I just don't give a fuck about shit right now."

"So, what's on the agenda?"

"I gotta get this money later on. I got a little business meeting and I could use your presence."

"Umm, damn, God! I gotta meet Pistola for some shit. It's important too. Can't you reschedule?"

"Nigga, really? You've been inactive for that long? Since when do you reschedule some shit like that?"

The two were intentionally a little vague on the phone, but they understood one another.

"True, indeed. You're right. I can't reschedule my shit either."

"You know what it is. I'll be alright. I got soldiers. Are you good? I could lend you a few."

"It's not that kind of situation."

Supreme responded with a warning yet a sarcastic tone, "Okay, you ol' Jason Bourne face; ol' Secret Service face nigga! I hope you ain't still dressing like you in a Wu Tang video!"

"That's better than dressing like a fucking fifteen year old, tight ass pants!"

"Nigga, I don't wear tight pants! Anyway, listen. I've been thinking about all the clothes, the book and legal money shit you've been talking about. I think that shit is a smart idea. You know, with the strength we got in the streets, we could get into the music business too. After this last flip we gonna switch things around."

"That's peace, God! Yeah, God, we going to elevate. Let's just take care of this shit real quick."

"Just wanted you to know I'm starting to think differently."

"That's what's up! Love you, bro! I'ma hit you later to make sure everything went well."

"Love you more. One!"

It was a pleasant feeling for Supreme to know that he had at least one true friend left. He quickly wiped his tears away and began preparing for his business meeting with Kendu and Don-Don.

******

Freedom wanted to tell Supreme the truth. He wanted to tell him exactly what he had planned for Pistola. But Supreme wasn't the same. His brother had changed. He stopped dreaming, and perhaps this slight change of heart was for the good. Or, it might be the desperate cry of an addict with nowhere to turn. Freedom couldn't figure it out. He just knew that he would come back for his brother when he could, and he prayed that Supreme would make it through the night.

CHAPTER 33

THE ART OF DECEPTION

IT was a squatter house across the street from South Jamaica Houses a.k.a. the 40 Projects. You could always tell when Kendu was home because the music was loud. And if his wife was there, her voice was stronger than a 1,000 watt amplifier.

"...I told you about coming over here, Stacey! This is *my* trap house!"

"Fuck outta here, nigga! This is your hoe house! I pay all the bills. What kinda trappin' is you doing?" Stacey yelled, pointing her finger in Kendu's face which further enraged him.

"Bitch, touch me again, I'ma fuck you up!"

"Who... what? Fuck who up?" She picked up her cell phone. "You know what? I got somebody for your ass! You want to keep putting your hands on me—"

Before she could complete her phone call, Kendu slapped her across the face with a broad open palm. He considered it merciful being that he didn't directly connect with her face; rather he smacked the hand holding her cell phone which sent her careening across the kitchen floor, and shattering her phone on the tiles. "Now tell that nigga you was gonna call to come do something! Pop off, bitch! You always provoking me!"

Kendu's mind was distraught. He was bipolar and couldn't rationalize that he should not be hitting her no matter how cuckoo she was.

Stacey was dazed, and from her perspective, the kitchen was spinning. She stumbled to stand and get her bearings. The blow was so stunning that her ears were ringing, so she couldn't make out his words as he went from slander to guilty apologies.

"Babe, are you okay, babe?"

Oh, she was okay. She was okay enough to quickly grab a bottle of Clorox off the kitchen counter and splash the contents into Kendu's eyes, blinding him. Then she completely blacked out, throwing glasses, cups and plates at her blind adversary as he stumbled forward and fell down, only to cut his hands on broken glass on the way up.

Kendu was no longer blind. His rage had consumed him.

He squinted through the burning sensation.

The word "temper" has many origins, but the oldest is its Latin root, "temperance", which means to discipline or restrain oneself. This gave birth to the Old English word, "temprain", meaning to bring something to its proper form or function by mixing it with something. Now, this shows that all words with the "temp" prefix sort of refer to some sort of time measure to bring about something. Temperature rises; steel must be tempered, and tempers tend to flare once limits are reached. Some tempers can become uncontrollable and almost trance-like.

For a person like Kendu who was emotionally and mentally unstable, it was easy for his limit to be reached. In his fit of vexation, the idea of remorse or pulling his punches had all but completely evacuated his thoughts. It was like watching a professional fighter pound on the schoolyard wimp.

Stacey had heart. She tried her best to fight back, but to no avail. Kendu pummeled her. He was not a small man; more than a 200 plus pound bruiser whose blows have brought many grown men to their knees.

That poor women curled over as she was devastated with rib-cracking blows. Kendu could not get control of himself. He rammed his elbow across her face and brought her face to his knee in a Muay Thai style clench. Stacey's body spun to the floor and flopped like a rag doll.

Kendu, in his hysterical tirade, continued to repeat the same thing over and over again. "Why you keep provoking me? Why you keep provoking me? Huh?" Then, he realized that the worst had happened.

Stacey lay there limp, dead and lifeless. She wasn't breathing. Her eyes still held onto his. Her last plea for help will never leave his mind. He spoke out loud, as though she could still hear him: "You do know this is your fault. You couldn't stop talking. Shit, I got too much shit going on for this bullshit."

He wrapped her body in a shower curtain and placed it in the tub. He rushed to try and tidy himself up so he didn't look like he just murdered a woman. He mumbled incessantly, murmuring insecurities and doubt. His constant sniffing only heightened his aggression and paranoia.

When his cell phone rang he spun around and almost shot it. "Yes, hello. Detective Rivera?"

"Yeah, it's me. Bring your ass outside."

"Muthafucka, you crazy? You trying to get me killed?"

"Chill out, *papi*. I'm in my regular civilian vehicle. Trust me, you're okay."

"You sure?"

"Aye, what the hell! You only got one day, and then you can fly to Hawaii and live the life. You know what? Since you feel so nervous, I'll come inside."

Kendu thought about Stacey and quickly reassessed the risk. "I'll just come outside. Fuck it!" he said, and scrambled to get outside.

Detective Rivera had been in a particularly good mood, as he was closing in on cracking his case. He knew that Supreme and Don-Don were the heads of two major crews that were ravishing Jamaica, Queens. What made it an even sweeter victory that he could taste on the tip of his tongue was the fact that Detective Boyce had no idea. He could finally prove his superiority as an officer. He had gone behind Boyce's back weeks prior and procured a witness protection deal for Kendu.

"Hola jefe! My favorite *rata!"* Rivera greeted Kendu as he got into his car.

"I ain't no *rata!"*

"Oh, stop it, *papi*. You got to embrace who you are. The world is filled with *ratas*. It's part of the natural pecking order."

"Why the fuck you got on all this Yankees shit in Queens, nigga? Fuck around and get a bullet in that Yankee fitted."

"I can't help myself, *papi*. I'm a Puerto Rican from the Bronx."

"Okay, well then I understand." Kendu was procrastinating, and the anxiety and nervousness had all but consumed him.

"Papa, it's fifty-five degrees and you're sweating like a dog. You gotta stay dry. If you soak your shirt, they might see the wire. Aww, come on! What happened to your face, *papi?"*

"Stacey. The bitch is crazy."

"Okay. I don't know why y'all don't just break up. She's fucking *loco*. You sure she ain't Boricua? Just don't kill her."

Kendu lifted up his red Rotten Apple shirt with the words "Welcome to South Jamaica, Queens" written across it to allow Rivera to tape the wire to his belly and chest. "Detective Rivera, can I ask you something? Are you sure no one will be able to find me?"

"We change your name, birthday and Social Security number. Being a confidential informant can be a lucrative business. You don't have to necessarily run and hide. You can stay in the field. You can hustle, get money, and fuck bitches as long as you continue to give me big fish to fry. We pay too. You can make a lot of money. "

"You mean be a professional rat?!"

"No, no. More like being an 'honorary detective' who goes deep under cover. Just something to consider. You remember the job, right? We just need to know when the drugs and money are to be exchanged. We don't need dialogue. A couple of kilos and a couple thousand dollars will give us enough to take them off the streets. What're the code words?"

"I gotta shit."

"Perfect! Remember, if it gets hectic, use the code words!"

Later That Day:

"...I hear the voice in the back of my mind like Mack,
Tighten up your circle before they hurt you.
Read their body language.
Eighty-five percent communication nonverbal,
Eighty-five percent swear they know you..."

"Feel It in the Air" by Beanie Sigel

Ironically, the song played low in Supreme's car speakers, but it spoke to his soul and became the theme song of the moment.

They swerved down Liberty avenue in his all black BMW. Supreme was a veteran when it came to situations like this. He drove with Kendu in the passenger seat, while Elmo and Smoke were off in the distance, covering the rear in an old raggedy indistinct Honda Accord '98 model. Elmo and Smoke were the contingency plans. They were to kill if things went wrong.

The black BMW slowed down after turning onto Dunkirk right off of Liberty Avenue. They pull up to an open space on a quiet dark back street just off of Dunkirk and parallel to a strip of mostly vacant warehouses. It was the perfect place to do a "deal and dash", and that single road connected directly from the St. Albans side of Queens to Hollis or Jamaica Avenue, and major highways. It was ideal for ditching the authorities.

A tinted out smoke gray Rav-4 Jeep pulled up behind them. Don-Don was playing it smart. He brought a vehicle that wouldn't attract attention.

The night was extra dark with only a speck of dim light coming from a crescent moon, which has many symbolic connotations. It can be looked at as a symbol of rebirth, or death. On that night it didn't represent anything positive.

Kendu and Supreme exited the vehicle with a book bag full of money.

Don-Don, Bulla and Magnum walk towards them. Bulla openly carried his 45-caliber handgun.

"Yo, Kendu! Who dem two niggas wit' him? Them niggas ain't Haitian, Kendu!" Supreme said, mumbling under his breath. "This shit don't feel right. Them niggas ain't got no bags in their hands. What the fuck did you bring me to?"

Meanwhile, Bulla said to Magnum, "Me see dat idiot bwoy Supreme now. We afi kill 'em."

"No, mon. Easy. Let we tek de money first, den brush 'em, nuh?" Don-Don interrupted. "That would be the wisest choice."

The two groups met face to face.

"So, y'all ready?" Don-Don asked Supreme.

"Yes, we're ready. Well, where the fuck are the drugs at? 'Cause the money's right here."

"In the car."

Supreme drew his gun and said, "You know what? You're trying to play with me. This don't feel right. Where are the fucking drugs?!" He dropped the bag of money and pulled out a second gun, keeping one aimed at Bulla and the other at Don-Don. "Yo, why the fuck y'all old Jamaican niggas look so familiar?" He rocked back and forth. He was on edge, and felt "Lady Death" gallivanting in the moonlight.

"Supreme, relax, nigga! You gonna fuck shit up!" Kendu said.

Supreme then turned one of his guns on Kendu. His eyes were roving to watch everyone in an attempt to interpret the next move.

Magnum raised his gun and yelled, "Yuh know me, pussy clot bwoy! Yuh and Freedom kill my lickle nephew, Fire!"

"Fire!" The name echoed in Supreme's head as a million flashes of childhood memories raced through his mind, abruptly stopping at the night he snapped Fire's neck.

The temperature had risen, and everyone's guns were drawn, except for Kendu and Don-Don's.

"Wait! Before y'all get all crazy, I gotta take a shit!" Kendu shouted.

It turned into an absolute calamity with a medley of gunfire.

Supreme let loose, shooting at Magnum while stooping down for the bag of cash. Both Magnum and Bulla were gunning for him so he took cover behind his BMW. Hollow slugs ripped through the steel and carbon fiber frame.

Don-Don pulled his .38 from its holster, while Kendu slowly backpedaled to remove himself from the situation, completely abandoning Supreme, leaving him for the wolves.

Abruptly, Elmo and Gun Smoke sped around the corner and flanked the three Caribbean gunmen. Supreme used that moment to get out of the line of fire.

Don-Don instantly dropped from a head shot from Gun Smoke's firearm. He lay on the ground dead from a bullet to the brain, but his nervous system still continued to make his body twitch as the last bit of life exited.

The entire scene was chaotic.

Bulla and Magnum were experienced, so they didn't go down as easily as Don-Don.

Supreme ran out of bullets and took off running while Bulla gave chase.

Magnum let loose, firing and reloading as he ducked behind the Rav-4. But he was clearly outgunned.

Elmo covered Smoke while he moved in for the kill. But before he could go for Magnum, Warrior sped by on an all black Kawasaki Ninja motorbike and lit up the entire block with a Mac-11, hitting young Elmo in his back and turning his fragile, young lanky frame into Swiss cheese. He flopped onto the cement like a discarded scarecrow. He then lay there in a puddle of blood, and quickly hemorrhaged and died from multiple gunshot wounds.

The night was still dark. All Supreme could do was get out of

Dodge, and he ran down Hilburn Avenue with his mind racing. He heard sirens in the background and saw the blue and red police lights through every gap in the bushes of the tree lined back streets. He got as far away as possible and tossed his gun in a dumpster. Everything had exploded in his face. He kept thinking that this wouldn't have happened if he had Freedom with him.

Off in the distance he heard the gunfire stop. It must have been all over until he felt numbness in his leg. When he stopped to look down, he saw his denim pants soaked in blood. He had taken a bullet to his leg and didn't realize it. He was limping, trying to make his way to Farmers Boulevard. He pulled his cell phone from his pocket and thought, *"I gotta call Freedom."*

Suddenly, he heard, "Aye, pussy clot bwoy! Ya feel ya safe? Yuh tek bad mon fi joke t'ing Bulla? Nah, bumbaclot joke t'ing." Bulla had silently stalked Supreme to catch him at the right moment.

Supreme turned around in a calm, stoic manner, as though to embrace his fate and without a remote attempt at defying the inevitable. A slug from Bulla's .44-caliber spun him around.

Bulla stood over his bleeding adversary.

"Fuck you, and fuck Fire! I don't give a fuck, motherfucker! I ripped his head off his fucking shoulders! Now shoot me, pussy!" Supreme shouted with blood and saliva spewing from his mouth in a final act of defiance while Bulla stood over him, execution style.

******

Smoke and Magnum shot it out with the Narcs who had arrived. They were simply outmanned with no chance of escape. They formed a temporary union. The two adversaries stood side by side, gun for gun against their common foe. They went out in a blaze of glory, dying side by side. The officers were vicious with retribution, unloading multiple gunshots into their pulverized corpses.

******

Fire's death ached Bulla to the core of his being, so the chance— the moment he gets to avenge his son is a moment he revels in. He rarely ever got to feel a sense of purpose unless he was killing. He leaned over Supreme and looked him straight in his eyes.

"Freeze!" Detective Rivera yelled. "I hate that piece of shit just as much as you do, but don't do it!"

Bulla had waited over a decade to let Fire's soul rest in peace, and Detective Rivera was snatching the moment of triumph away from his grasp. "Nah, mon. Nah, mon. Mon afi dead!" he snarled as he looked at Rivera with a long, cold hard stare. His eyes were intense beady pieces of black charcoals.

Time froze, and a brief millisecond felt like an eon.

Detective Rivera screamed, "Drop the fucking weapon!" But Bulla was lost in a trance of a bloodthirsty rage.

Supreme was in shock, and every single cell in his being commanded him to move, to get up, to run, but he couldn't. He was at Bulla's mercy. Supreme was at peace with his fate. His heart raced and pounded against his chest like a drum. With every passing moment the pounding became louder and louder. He knew he was no saint. He knew the consequences of his lifestyle. He closed his eyes and prepared to dance with Karma.

Bulla's clenched his index finger, but before he could completely squeeze and fire, Detective Rivera pumped three bullets into his frail slender chest, throwing him back three feet. His body went limp and crashed up against a sycamore tree, splattering blood onto the grass.

He died before his body hit the ground. Eerily, his eyes stayed open like windows into the great beyond.

It wasn't Rivera's first time discharging his firearm, but it was his first time watching the life leave a man's body. The image of Bulla's bullet ridden frame contorted and disfigured would forever haunt his mind.

He would have to live with the idea that another indigenous brother was murdered, and the blood was on his hands.

Supreme lay there wounded, walking that thin tightrope, balancing on the borderline between life and death. He faded in and out of consciousness while other officers handcuffed his war scarred wrists. He was fading away as everything he loved flashed before his eyes. Before he completely drifted off into the dark abyss of oblivion, one single mantra played over and over in his head: *"Kendu set me up… Kendu set me up…"* Like a sad love song, the volume slowly faded into obscurity.

THE ELEGY

A T 2:40 am in the morning, Sopa notified Pistola to come to the Botanica on Broadway across the street from Fort Tryon Park with his delivery.

A thunderstorm was brewing as the final days of summer were coming to an end.

Sopa craved revenge. He longed to see Freedom cowering on his knees. He had plans for Freedom, and so did Gato.

Sopa sat behind the counter awaiting Pistola's arrival. It was late, so the gate was halfway down. He had Joselito on the corner of Arden and Broadway playing lookout, while Flako and El Gato were in back sitting behind a hidden door. El Gato was wearing an all black short sleeve H&M shirt. He twirled an eight inch dagger around in his hand. Flako was silent and still. Everyone was awaiting the guest of honor.

The smell of frankincense and myrrh mixed with the aroma of patchouli oil smoke filled the air. The Botanica is supposed to be a place to purchase spiritual supplies, and a sort of neutral ground for folks who may study a variety of what may be considered pagan practices. However, on that day there was nothing neutral about the Botanica located on Broadway and Arden.

Sopa's phone rang. It was Joselito. *"Que?"* he asked.

"Pistola is here, and it looks like he's got the package."

Sopa grinned and hung up the phone.

******

Pistola drove up and found a perfect parking spot right in front of the Botanica. He had Freedom tied up in his trunk, something he thought would never happen. Before getting out, he said a quick prayer to himself. He had done a lot of crimes and was an efficient mercenary. Who else could put Freedom in a trunk? But despite having years of experience, he still got nervous once in a while.

Sopa and Freedom were like father figures to him so it hurt to be in the middle of their conflict. But he was given an ultimatum—a choice as a matter of fact. The two adversaries could not co-exist in the same space and time. Someone had to die. He was merely playing the catalyst that would expedite a speedy resolution. It was an extremely peculiar place for him, but he was forced to choose, so he did.

Pistola forcefully grabbed Freedom and assisted him out of the trunk. Freedom's hands were tied behind his back and an extra-large hoody covered his blindfolded eyes and gagged mouth. He slapped Freedom in the back of his head and ordered, "Hurry the fuck up!" Then he firmly pressed the barrel of his gun against the small of Freedom's back, nudging him forward. He cautiously looked around before pushing Freedom's head down before they ducked underneath the half open gate. "Duck, *estupido!*" he ordered.

Opening the door, Sopa was there to welcome him. "*Hola, Negrito!* I thought I'd never see you again!" he said in a sarcastic tone.

Freedom scowled when he heard the all too familiar voice of his captor.

Sopa moved slow and deadly like a slithering cobra until his lips were about an inch away from Freedom's ear.

As he drew closer, sweat began to pour off of Freedom's brow, and his breath became shorter and faster.

Sopa's whisper was like the hissing of a snake. "You're big and strong now. Too bad all those muscles couldn't save her. I heard she moaned like a little whore. She begged for it. But don't worry. I didn't fuck her," he snickered. "My friend Gato did the honors. I don't like old pussy. When I'm done killing you, I'ma fuck your daughter! Hell, I might bring her here so I can fuck her in front of you!" Then he delivered a deafening slap to the side of Freedom's head, and followed it up with an uppercut.

Pistola pressed his gun into Freedom's ribs before Freedom could even think to fall.

Sopa turned to Pistola and said, "I'm proud of you. Very impressed. I didn't think you'd pull this off."

Freedom tried to yell through the gag on his mouth.

"Pistola, I think Jamaal has something to say," Sopa said mockingly.

Pistola responded to Sopa's gesture and pulled the gag off of Freedom's mouth and took of the blindfold. "So, what do you have to say for yourself, Jamaal? And why are you crying?"

Freedom's eyes were like jet black pearls. His hatred started to heat up like a furnace until it morphed into an inferno. "Are you alone?" he asked.

"What kind of stupid question is that? Oh, you want to meet your lady's other man? Okay, I'll introduce you. Don't worry. He likes boys too!"

Freedom smiled. "You want to know why I'm crying? I'm crying because at first I thought that something was wrong with me. I thought I needed to change. I thought I was evil. Now I understand that a little evil can be very necessary."

In an unforeseen turn of events, Pistola turned his gun on Sopa.

Freedom untied his own hands and grabbed a gun from Pistola's back. He quickly put his hand over Sopa's mouth. Now the tide was turned, and the once mighty cobra was the prey. "Shh! Now, where is Gato?" Freedon whispered.

Pistola began tying Sopa's hands…

******

Earlier that Night:

"Why the fuck ain't Supreme picking up his phone?" Freedom complained while sitting in the passenger seat of Pistola's black I-35 Infiniti.

"Wassup wit' 'Preme, papa?"

"I don't know. He was supposed to do some shit tonight, but fuck it! I just hope he's alright."

"Freedom, you sure you want to do it like this?"

"Yep. I don't want him to suspect anything. I know Sopa. He's got to feel like he's in complete control in order for him to let his guard down."

"Yeah, he's dangerous. That's why we should run in and just fuckin' kill 'em all."

"Yeah, Pistola, but we don't know what kinda artillery they're working with or how many soldiers they got."

"I feel you."

"Plus, I know Sopa's work. He didn't kill Samaya, he just ordered the hit. This shit is personal. I want the motherfucker that did that to her."

"Okay, brother. You have my loyalty. You know I'm going to have to make this look as convincing as possible."

"I know."

"One last thing, Freedom… do you trust me?"

"Actually, I don't. I just trust *me*." Freedom was a very stoic man on a mission. He had to be confident in his decision. This wasn't his first time riding in the trunk of someone's car, but at least this time he'd be conscious, he thought.

Some people see better with their eyes closed. Being blindfolded and curled up in the trunk, there was a sense of solitude. You can't imagine how much we are over-saturated daily with multi-forms of stimuli, from music, TV, billboards, etc. Then, even when we sit in the dark and silence, what about the mind? It wanders, it worries and it wonders. It is hardly ever quiet.

The blindfold and the dark forced Freedom to look inward. He was curled up in a fetal position as though he was a developing child, and the trunk was the embryonic sack.

Then he saw it. He saw the blood; he heard the drums; he felt the ancestors' blades, machetes, and they spun around in his head. He heard the drums, and he heard the remnants of Samaya's voice: *"I am with you!"*

For a brief millisecond Freedom felt comfort and relief, but as comforting as the spirit can be, we are still charged with the work.

He had found the very meaning of his name and by forgiving himself while in that trunk— in that "embryonic sac"—he had been reborn with one solitary truth. Karma is subject to guilt, and guilt is based on your moral standard. Freedom didn't feel guilty for anything except for Samaya's death.

******

Freedom pulled Sopa in close and checked him for any weapons. "Pistola, pass me the machete, and keep this motherfucker at bay," he instructed, and began to move towards the back door. He signaled to Pistola to take the lead.

Freedom then kicked the door open, and Pistola walked in with one arm around Sopa's neck, and the other hand pressing the barrel of his .45 caliber Desert Eagle pressed against Sopa's temple.

Flako and Gato were both caught off guard and had no idea that this was going to happen.

Sopa angrily blurted out, *"Coño! Mata los!"*

Freedom calmly chimed in, "No, don't listen to him. That will just get you murdered quicker." In his left hand he wielded the machete, and in his right was a Glock 9-mm. He turned to Pistola and said, "Tie Sopa up in that chair. I want him to watch."

Pistola took the same rope that he had loosely tied Freedom with and used it on Sopa, who continued to taunt the young immature Pistola.

"Do you know what happened *a tu madre*, Pistola? She was a disloyal little whore, just like her bastard son!"

"Pistola, don't listen to him. He's trying to get in your head."

Flako slowly but gradually reached for his weapon, but Freedom had been in this space before. He was keenly aware and alert. Sopa was chattering, Flako was flinching, and Gato was inching forward. Freedom had to take control of the scenario quickly, and he did, hitting both men with a shot to their legs and causing them to stumble to the ground. This didn't prevent Flako from continuing to reach, but his reflexes were too slow.

"Shoot him, Flako!" Sopa shouted.

Freedom immediately gave Flako eight more shots to his head, disfiguring his long, sharp-ridged face. Each slug chipped away at his skull as though he was being rapidly dismantled like a jigsaw puzzle made of muscle, bone and tendons.

Then Freedom stared directly into Gato's eyes as he lay there on the ground nursing his wound.

Gato was not a man of many words, but Sopa was. "That was a stupid move, Jamaal. You must want to go to jail, because those shots definitely woke up the neighbors." Sopa had no heart. Nothing fazed him. "So, Pistola…"

"What do you want?" Pistola asked, pointing his gun in Sopa's direction.

"I killed your whore mother!"

Those words spewed like acid, and Pistola's mind quickly went back to all the fond memories he had of his mother as a child. Truly, the only joyful memories he really had were when he was with her. He was young when his mother was murdered. His gun hand shook with anxiety.

"Shut the fuck up, Sopa, before I chop your head off! You know what? Let's get this over with!" Freedom yelled, and turned to Gato as he lay there squirming in pain. "Now, you must be Gato. Don't that mean 'cat' in Spanish? So, you must have nine lives, huh?" He took aim but stopped.

Gato raised his hand as though to block the bullet. "Please, don't!"

"So, you can speak English. Okay. And you're a lefty, huh? Stick out your left hand."

Gato hesitated, and that infuriated Freedom even more. "Hold out your fucking hand!" Hatred, anger and pure unadulterated rage were so ferocious it consumed every part of him. His heart was a volcano erupting with sorrow, and his veins were channels that distributed the pain as hot lava ran through him. His thirst for blood could only be quenched by the poisonous taste of revenge.

Freedom gave Gato a swift slice with the edge of the machete, causing his wrist to open a major vein. Bright red blood spewed from Gato's left wrist. "Oh my God! Shit!" he screamed as he groveled in pain.

Sopa seemed enraged by his comrade's lack of fortitude. "*Coño, maricon!* Stop fucking bitching! If they kill you, then they kill you. But stop fucking crying and die like a man!"

Freedom said, "Oh, Sopa! Aren't you the motivational speaker. How does it feel to bleed, you fucking coward? You disgraced the one thing that I loved. You like to cut folks, huh?"

He then stepped in front of Gato. "Don't worry, papa. Mr. Gato, I'm not like you. I'm not a butcher. Too much blood makes me nauseous. Now, give me your right hand.

"Pistola, are you going to let him kill me? Huh? Kill your father?" Sopa asked.

"What?"

"You heard me. I'm your father! Yes, you have my blood in you!"

"No! That's not true!"

Their back and forth argument was interrupted by nine consecutive gunshots as Freedom let off rounds all around the room.

He saved the final shot for the side of Gato's head. Gray matter and little chips of bone mixed with blood splattered on the floor. Freedom then placed the gun in Gato's right hand. He needed the murder to look like a suicide.

He turned his attention towards Sopa, whose cell phone was ringing consistently. Freedom dug into Sopa's pocket, grabbed the phone and pressed the talk button. *"Viejito, mira policia! Policia! Vaminos! Vaminos rapido, papa!"* Freedom heard Joselito shouting over the phone. His eyes opened wide. He could hear the sirens in the far distance.

"Freedom, what are we gonna do?" Pistola asked anxiously.

Sopa was one of the most resourceful men ever. He had been slowly but surely easing the ropes from around his wrists. He was only chattering to distract them. He needed the opportune time to escape his bonds, and in the midst of the confusion he had a brief window to capitalize from it.

To Pistola's shock, Sopa sprang to his feet, flung the chair at Freedom, then charged Pistola like a extremely agile sumo wrestler and slammed him on his back, stunning him. He wrestled with Pistola, took his .45 and quickly scrambled to his feet. "Good-bye, *niño!"*

Pistola wasn't the best fighter, and wasn't quick or skilled enough to reclaim his gun. He tried to stand up, and his sudden move was met with three shots to his body that threw him back to the floor, and his soul swiftly left his 175 pound frame. He died with his eyes wide open.

Sopa then let off a couple of shots at Freedom as he charged out the door.

"Damn, Pistola!" Freedom thought as he simultaneously gave chase.

When Sopa got outside, Freedom heard one loud gunshot. He quickly ran outside of the Botanica and was utterly shocked to see his daughter Rain standing over Sopa with a smoking gun in her hand. "What the fuck!" he exclaimed.

Rain spoke in a rapid murmur, as though she was someone possessed. "I tracked his businesses. He has a bunch of LLC's (limited liability corporations). There was one called 'Spirit Works LLC', and it turned out to be this place."

Freedom was in a time warp standing over Sopa's body as blood gurgled from his punctured lung.

The sirens wailed as they drew closer and closer.

There standing in front of Freedom was an angel. Rain didn't understand the magnitude of what she had done, but she was her father's child. His DNA ran through her veins. Her bright brown eyes cried out.

"What did you do? Come on. You gotta go!"

Then in the far off distance he heard the walkie-talkies broadcasting, *"We have Shots fired! Assault in progress!!! We need back up!!!!"*

Freedom had to be cunning, swift and resolute in his decision. There was no time for hesitation. The police were close. He thought, *"If we run and they find her, it could ruin her life. But my life is already ruined. I can't lose her too!"*

Then he heard the words of Ifa Abeyo: *"You will be faced with a choice. Protect that little girl!"* In that brief five seconds of space it felt like time had paused and stood still. He had to choose his daughter's life or his own. "Give me the gun and get the fuck home!" he told her.

"But... but Daddy..." and her tear ducts flooded as she stared at the man she had rejected and shunned, not knowing that his love ran so deep that he'd give his very life for hers.

He repeated himself one last time, extending his hand. "Give me the gun, now!" Once the gun was in his possession he said, "Now, run. Go home. I love you, Rain, and I'm sorry."

"But Daddy…"

"Go now! Get home!" He watched her run off in her gray sweat suit and hair wrapped in a scarf. There was no time for parenting or finding out how she got the gun. No, his paternal instincts kicked in. He did what he had to do.

"Put the fucking gun down!"

Freedom kept his back to the officers as they approached him with their weapons drawn and yelling at the top of their lungs. Before tossing the gun in front of him, he wiped it with his T-shirt just to be certain that Rain's fingerprints weren't on it.

"I said get the fuck down!"

Freedom was alone again. He could hear that inner voice; that inner voice that shrinks into the spacesuit that most call their body. He'd been through it before. First comes the state of equanimity, and then the numbness.

He laid flat on the concrete as the officers handcuffed him and had him on display like a runaway slave who had been captured. He stared off in the distance, looking at Sopa's body shaking and trembling. The sight of his nemesis slowly dying in front of him gave him pleasure, and he grinned. Oblivious to the arresting officers, their voices were mere shallow echoes off in the distance of his mind. His smile told a story of retribution and redemption. Even as he was brutishly tossed around, he silently rejoiced because his mission was complete. In his eyes was the electric fire. He was that rebellious field hand that would fight back no matter what. But on that night, not fighting was his best option. Despite the shoddy nature of the events, at least he saved his daughter. At least she found it in her heart to call him "Daddy".

******

Rain stared at the waning moon and wept a thousand tears. For every tear she shed, she wished she could just tell her Dad the one thing she hadn't told him in years… *"I love you!"*

THE END